MY INDIAN YEARS

1910–1916

LORD HARDINGE AS VICEROY

MY INDIAN YEARS
1910-1916

THE REMINISCENCES OF

LORD HARDINGE OF PENSHURST

K.G., P.C., G.C.B., G.C.S.I., G.C.M.G., G.C.I.E., G.C.V.O., LL.D

★

LONDON
JOHN MURRAY, ALBEMARLE STREET, W.

First Edition . . . *1948*

DS 480. 3 . H345

Made and Printed in Great Britain by Butler & Tanner Ltd., Frome and London

CONTENTS

ILLUSTRATIONS

★ *From " The Historical Record of the Imperial Visit to India, 1911," by permission of the High Commissioner of India.*

FOREWORD

IN an earlier volume entitled *Old Diplomacy*, Lord Hardinge of Penshurst recorded his reminiscences of his life in the Diplomatic Service during the period from 1880 to 1922, in the later years of which he played so prominent a part.

An interval in his remarkable Diplomatic career occurred when Lord Hardinge was appointed Viceroy of India in 1910 in succession to Lord Minto. This high office he held with great distinction until 1916, when he returned home and resumed the post of Permanent Under-Secretary of State for Foreign Affairs, which led to his taking part in the Peace negotiations and Treaties of 1919.

The present volume covers the 1910–16 period of Lord Hardinge's Viceroyalty, during which the burden of his anxieties and responsibilities was greatly increased by the outbreak of the First World War in 1914 and especially by the Mesopotamia campaign.

Lord Hardinge relates in his own words his views and experiences of those troublous times, giving a vivid picture of the unceasing toil, the problems, the pageantry as well as the pleasures and the pains of a Viceroy's life.

We read of the high hopes with which he set out from England, justly fortified with the pride of family tradition in following in the steps of his grandfather, who had gone out to India as Governor-General from 1844 to 1847.

One of Lord Hardinge's first preoccupations was to prepare for the great Coronation Durbar in Delhi in 1911, and, in the light of recent events in India, it is well to recall the momentous announcement, made on that occasion, of the transfer of the capital from Calcutta to that ancient city. History alone will judge the merits or otherwise of these weighty events here recorded.

FOREWORD

It is for others to assess the benefits attendant upon Lord Hardinge's administration in India : but it may unquestionably be asserted that by his tactful and friendly intercourse with the Ruling Princes of India, he won, in a quite exceptiona degree, their devoted loyalty and unfailing support.

The success of Lord Hardinge's early efforts to quell the prevailing sedition received a cruel setback when the attempt to assassinate him, which so nearly cost him his life, was made at the State Entry into Delhi in 1912.

In addition to this misfortune, Lord Hardinge was destined to suffer overwhelming personal sorrows in the loss of his dearly loved wife and, shortly afterwards, of his elder son, who succumbed to his wounds in the First World War. · Yet, despite these shattering blows, Lord Hardinge steadfastly and courageously carried on his duties in India—at the special request of the Government—beyond the normal span of Viceroyalty, until his return home in 1916.

CROMER.

January 1948.

CHAPTER I

THE BEGINNING OF MY VICEROYALTY

IT is difficult to state exactly when an idea begins to materialize into a definite ambition or aim, but surrounded as I was from my earliest childhood by Indian trophies, pictures and curiosities, an attentive listener to anecdotes of historic or personal interest connected with India, and with family traditions inspired by my nearest relations having all done service in that country, it is not surprising that, in my case, the transition from an indefinite idea to a definite ambition to go to India was a short one. Anyhow, it is an absolute fact that twenty years before I went to India, when I was merely occupying a subordinate position in the Diplomatic Service, my mind was made up that, although I hoped with some confidence to become in due course an Ambassador, my real ambition was to follow in the footsteps of my grandfather, the 1st Viscount Hardinge, who was Governor-General of India from 1844 to 1848, and to become one day Viceroy of India. I said so in 1890 when engaged to be married and I believed then, as I still believe, that one has only ardently and sufficiently to desire in order to attain the object of one's ambition, and my wife never forgot it.

It was when on a visit to Windsor in January 1909 as Permanent Under-Secretary of State for Foreign Affairs, that I was asked by my great friend Lord Knollys whether, if I was offered the succession to Lord Minto in India, I would accept it. This was nearly two years before the completion of Lord Minto's term of office. I replied that I would do so without hesitation since it was my highest ambition to go to India as Viceroy. Knollys mentioned the idea to the King, who expressed himself in favour of it at that time, and from that moment I was inwardly convinced that the offer would be made to me, though there was nothing I could do to promote my candidature. Nor could I foresee the opposition by the King that would arise later, the sad circumstances under which the offer would be made, and the tragic events that would beset my path after the realization of my ambition. Had I been able to see into the future I wonder if my sense of duty would have been sufficient to compel me to accept.

A year later, when it was becoming necessary to consider the appointment of a successor to Lord Minto, I learnt that Mr. Asquith, the Prime Minister, had suggested to King Edward my appointment as Viceroy, but the King objected, saying that he wished me to remain in England as I was useful to him at the Foreign Office. At the same time he urged strongly the appointment of Lord Kitchener as Viceroy. Mr. Asquith and Lord Morley, Secretary of State for India, were both resolutely opposed to Lord Kitchener's appointment as they considered it would be disastrous at that time to nominate a soldier to that position. They never wavered in their opposition. Shortly before the King left for Biarritz in February 1910, the question was again raised by His Majesty and with the same result. In the meantime Kitchener was pressing his own candidature and pulling all the strings to exert pressure upon Asquith and Morley, but without result.

It was on the King's return from Biarritz in April that the question of Minto's successor was reopened and Asquith again put forward and pressed for the acceptance of my name. The King, who was already ill as I was told afterwards, wrung his hands saying that my name was not to be put forward again, that he wished to keep me near him at the Foreign Office, and that if Asquith persisted in refusing to appoint Kitchener he must find some candidate other than myself for the post of Viceroy. Asquith remarked that it was not likely that I, a former Ambassador, would be content to remain indefinitely at the head of the Foreign Office, and that I would have a good claim to the

Embassy at Paris whenever that post should fall vacant. The King replied that he did not care and that if I went to the Embassy at Paris he would always be able to get hold of me at short notice whenever he wanted me. Asquith promised not to put forward my name again and I understood that the appointment of Sir George Murray, Permanent Under-Secretary at the Treasury, was seriously under discussion when other happenings occurred which changed entirely the trend of events.

Through the kindness of friends in and connected with the Cabinet I was kept well informed of the progress of the above events, but although the realization of my ambition to be Viceroy seemed for some months to be apparently hopeless, I had no doubt that I would secure the appointment in the end, though I never thought for one moment that it could possibly reach me through the death of my revered friend and benefactor, King Edward, to whose invariable kindness I am more indebted than to anybody else, whom I loved more than any man outside my family that I have ever known, and whose death was a terrible shock and sadness to me, such as I had then hardly known.

I twice saw the King after his death, lying in his bed in Buckingham Palace, the second time in the presence of Queen Alexandra. It was a very emotional interview that I can never forget. She sent me later as a souvenir a jade electric bell that I had so often seen on the King's writing-table and bearing his initials.

During those days I was too sad to think of India or the future in any way, but it was at Windsor when waiting with my wife in the sun on the lawn outside St. George's Chapel for the arrival of the funeral procession that Lord Morley came up to us, and taking me aside asked if I would like to succeed Lord Minto as Viceroy of India. I told him that to do so would be the realization of the dream of my life. What struck me as curious at the time was that the only question he put to me was whether I was

3

a free-trader, and I was honestly able to say that I was then and always had been a free-trader. He told me that I might regard the matter as settled, but that I was to tell nobody except my wife. Of course I was overjoyed at knowing that my dream had at last come true, but at the same time I could not help feeling that I would have much preferred that the offer had been made to me on some other occasion less closely associated with my late King and Master, though I was convinced that under the altered circumstances he would not have opposed but would have approved my appointment.

It was not till the 10th June that I received a charming letter from Asquith offering me officially the appointment, which of course I readily accepted. During those intervening three weeks I had the time of my life as I heard the question of Lord Minto's successor frequently discussed at dinner tables, and although my name was sometimes mentioned as having some chance, it was generally considered that I had but little in view of Kitchener's candidature. On the other hand, there is no doubt that Kitchener himself had misgivings and he tried to discourage me by sending me a message through Sir Walter Lawrence, Curzon's Private Secretary in India, to the effect that it was impossible to fill the post satisfactorily unless one had at least £8,000 a year of private fortune. Lawrence told him, and me later, that his statement was quite untrue and that he himself was in the best position to know this. My after experience proved that he was correct. My appointment was published on the 11th June and it was a bitter blow to Kitchener. He disappeared entirely for ten days to hide his disappointment, nobody knowing where he had gone. It must have been very galling, for he had counted on it so surely that he had actually appointed his staff, whose names I knew.

It was at the meeting of the Privy Council at St. James's Palace after the funeral of King Edward that King George asked me to come to see him afterwards at Marlborough House. The King knew all that had passed between Asquith and his late father and was very nice about it. He told me quite frankly that he was and always had been in favour of Kitchener's candidature, but that since the Government had decided with his assent that the next Viceroy was to be myself and not Kitchener, he assured me that as such I could always count on his full confidence and warm support. He told me at the same time how much he valued and appreciated the loyal services I had always rendered to his father.

In July 1910 I was raised to the Peerage against my will. I would have liked to go to India as Sir Charles Hardinge, just as my grandfather had gone as Sir Henry Hardinge, and I would gladly have accepted a peerage at the conclusion of my term of office. But the King would not hear of this, and as I wished to preserve my family name so as to make the family connection clear to India, I assumed, with my brother's assent, the title I now bear.

As I did not leave for India till the beginning of November, I retained my post at the Foreign Office till then, but my presence there was irregular owing to the many preparations I had to make before leaving England for a period of five years, which in the end was extended to five and a half years. There were many people who told me that it would be impossible for me to take out with me my little daughter Diamond who was just ten years old, but happily I met Lord Lansdowne, who told me that it was all nonsense and that he had had his daughter, Lady Waterford, during the whole of his Viceroyalty when she was about the same age as Diamond. This decided me, for it was bad enough as it was to have to leave in England my two sons, the elder at Sandhurst and the younger at Harrow.

I was also concerned as to my financial position in India, and Lord Curzon, to enlighten me, invited me to Hackwood, where he showed me an enormous ledger containing all the accounts of his Viceroyalty, written in his own hand ! No wonder he had to work fourteen hours a day. I was quite reassured and still more so when Lord Lansdowne told me that during his term of office in India he had saved £20,000 of his salary. I may mention here that during the whole of my time in India I saw my accounts only once, and then from curiosity. There is an experienced staff of clerks to manage the Viceroy's official and personal expenditure under the control of the Military Secretary who informed me at the end of each month of the situation of my finances, which was always satisfactory, since the post of Viceroy is one of the very few where the salary is sufficient to cover necessary expenditure.

One of my greatest trials during these months was the making of speeches at two public dinners given to me by the County of Kent and old Harrovians. In the Diplomatic Service speechifying is not encouraged, and I know of instances where Ambassadors have "put their foot into it" when making a speech. Consequently I had had no practice in speaking and it was hard to begin doing so at the age of 52. I passed successfully through this ordeal, but although I have since had to make innumerable speeches in India and elsewhere, it has always been to me a source of difficulty to speak in public. However, my speech to the County of Kent was the most important of the two and received the warm approval of the Government. Sir E. Grey wrote me a charming letter. He said : " You made a first-rate speech to the ' men of Kent '. The whole of it seemed to me to be laid on good strong lines. . . . I am delighted that you are now launched so successfully before the public eye. This sounds as if you were a new Dreadnought, and if public men were ships, that is what you could now be." I think I appreciated this compliment more than any other paid to me at that time.

M. Sazonow, Russian Minister for Foreign Affairs, also sent me a telegram expressing the thanks of the Russian Government for my friendly references in my speech to Russia and promising to co-operate with me in a friendly settlement of any question arising to affect Anglo-Russian relations in India.

On the eve of my departure Winifred and I lunched with the King and Queen to take farewell of them, and the King conferred upon me the Grand Crosses of the Star of India and of the Indian

Empire, and the Order of the Crown of India on Winifred. The Foreign Office also gave me a farewell dinner and a beautiful dressing case to which forty-eight of them had subscribed. It was with great regret that I severed my connection with Sir E. Grey and the Foreign Office, where I had spent a very happy period of nearly six years of absorbing interest, almost the most interesting years of my life, and where I felt all were the most loyal friends.

It was on the 2nd of November that we left for India with Du Boulay, my invaluable Private Secretary and two A.D.C.s, Major Fraser of the Scots Guards and Captain Forrester of the Grenadiers, two of the nicest and best that ever man had. I had appointed Lieut.-Colonel Maxwell, V.C., and Major Mackenzie, both of the Indian Army, as my Military Secretary and Controller respectively, and they were to meet me in India. There was a great crowd at the station to see us off and much amusement was created by the fact that I was so busy saying good-bye to my friends that the train actually went off without me, but after much signalling and whistling was eventually brought back to the platform. But even then I was nearly left behind and climbed into the train as it was starting for the second time.

I left England full of enthusiasm for my great undertaking and more than happy at the complete realization of my highest ambition. I appreciated fully the immense difficulties before me and the heavy responsibilities of the office I was to hold. I recalled that my own grandfather must have felt as I was feeling and that in the face of great trials and dangers he had achieved lasting success, and I hoped I might have the strength, wisdom and courage to do the same. I was fully aware of my own limitations and was very diffident, though not afraid. Had I known all that was to befall me before I set foot again on the shores of England, how different my feelings would have been from what they were on that November morning. What a mercy it is that the future is a closed book.

We had a very pleasant and uneventful journey as far as Port

Said, where we were met by my old friend and colleague, Sir Ronald Graham, who gave us dinner at the hotel. We drove round the town in a carriage lent by the Governor whom I visited later. He was an ex-Balliol undergraduate and an advanced nationalist. Port Said struck me as a very poor and dishevelled place, but the journey through the Canal was full of interest and Diamond was thrilled at the sight of the Arabs and their camels, etc. The Red Sea was hot but pleasant and we were greatly interested by the number of sharks round the ship and by the whales and flying fish.

On arrival at Aden I assumed, as is usual, the attributes of the Viceroy and hoisted the Viceroy's flag, which was saluted by the shore batteries and by an Italian cruiser which had received orders from the King of Italy to await and salute me on my arrival. When the Captain of the cruiser came on board I asked him to transmit my respectful thanks to the King of Italy, whom I had had the honour of meeting several times when travelling with King Edward and whom I then knew fairly well, for this exceptional act of courtesy. I sent my A.D.C., Captain Forrester, to return my visit and he came back an hour later with a flushed face, after having successfully held his own in spite of the overwhelming hospitality of the Italian wardroom officers on a very hot day.

We went on shore to a reception at the Residency and later, when the temperature was cooler, we drove to see the Crater and the old fortifications built by my grandfather when Governor-General, and we passed through the town of Aden, visiting the water tanks, a wonderful engineering feat of which no records exist but which are said to have been built by the Queen of Sheba. During our drive we were escorted by a squadron of the Aden Camel Corps and I remember well how mysterious it seemed that, although there were about twenty camels in the escort, there was absolutely no sound of their feet on the sandy roads.

I received a visit from the Sultan of Lahej, who brought me several bags of excellent Mocha coffee.

8

Aden is a desolate place, but very healthy in spite of the dirty conditions of the population. The British troops do well there in spite of the heat, but I cannot help thinking that that is largely due to the fact that they are always seasoned troops going home after a long spell in India and that they are heartened up by the idea of going home within the year. There had been trouble in a Mahratta regiment through the intrigues and influence of *one* Brahmin. The regiment was to be punished and the Colonel was dismissed. Since the war the troops have been withdrawn, except a detachment of artillery and air force.

The remainder of our journey through the Indian Ocean was very comfortable and we arrived at Bombay at 5.30 a.m. on November 18th, Admiral Sir Edmund Slade, an old friend, Commander-in-Chief on the East India Station, came on board with his staff at 7 a.m. We landed at 8 a.m. under a Royal Salute from H.M.S. *Hyacinth*. We were received on the steps of the Apollo Bunder by Sir G. Clarke, the Governor, and his wife and a vast number of officials, Ruling Chiefs and others. After taking our seats in a large tent and after the usual presentations an address of welcome was presented by the Municipality of Bombay, to which I replied. In their address a reference was made to my connection with India through my grandfather, Sir Henry Hardinge, who had landed there nearly seventy years before and to whose services to India many flattering references were made. In my reply I scored a point by remarking that I had an older and even closer connection with Bombay than through my grandfather, since I had been told that in the Cathedral there was a monument which, according to its inscription, was " erected by the public spirit of Bombay to consecrate the memory of Captain George Nicholas Hardinge of the Royal Navy " who fell in the hour of victory after a combat lasting three days and the capture of a large French frigate which had been the terror of the Indian Seas. This was my great-uncle and the naval engagement had taken place 102 years earlier. This statement of mine created quite a sensation, and the press was much amused by what they considered a score off the Municipality. The Bishop told me later that a great number of people had in consequence visited the Cathedral to see the monument. I also went to see it, and was much pleased to find that it is one of great beauty and artistic merit by Bacon in 1814 and by far the best monument in the Cathedral. In my reply to the address I made the further announcement, which I had only learnt by telegram on my arrival, that the King and Queen would hold an Imperial Durbar in India in December 1911. This prospect naturally created great enthusiasm throughout the whole of India.

Sir George and Lady Clarke received us at Government House with great hospitality and made us very comfortable. I was not impressed with Government House in Bombay, which enjoys a wonderful position on Europa Point, but which, with the exception of a few good reception rooms in a separate building, consists entirely of scattered bungalows. It is hardly a worthy or suitable residence for so important a personage as the Governor of a Province holding the gateway of India.

We left Bombay on the following day and arrived at Calcutta on the 21st November. I was much struck by the beauty and wonderful fertility of the country we traversed, while Diamond was thrilled at the sight of monkeys, camels and elephants. Whenever the train stopped the District Officers came to see me, and I was much impressed by their smartness and their self-reliance. I shall say more of these later.

We had a great reception at Calcutta, the streets being lined with troops and immense crowds everywhere. We were received at the foot of the steps of Government House by Lord and Lady Minto, the Commander-in-Chief, the Members of Council and all the high officials of State. As I entered the great marble hall the first picture to catch my eye was that of my grandfather, who seemed to be looking towards me, and I felt that this was of good omen.

The Mintos did not leave Calcutta till two days later, which was uncomfortable both for them and for me, for although I was not actually Viceroy until I had been sworn in, it was only natural that I should be treated on all sides as the rising and not the setting sun.

I made a mental resolution that when my turn came I would arrange otherwise. During those two days I had long talks with many Indians, and I began to feel that if only the trials for sedition then in progress, could be finished and set aside there might be some hope of peace. Curzon's policy of the partition of Bengal, to which the unrest was chiefly due, was severely criticized on all sides, but in those days I never held out the very slightest hope of the reversal of that policy. Still, even in Bengal there was a general feeling that, in view of the decision of the King to hold an Imperial Durbar in India in a year's time, peace was very desirable, and the hope was repeatedly mentioned that it would be the King who would reverse the partition of Bengal, a hope that was realized, although nothing was more improbable at that time.

Within an hour of being sworn in as Viceroy and Governor-General I had an interesting lesson as to the relative value of British and Indian troops for the preservation of order. The Lieutenant-Governor of Bengal, Sir E. Baker, came to see me and informed me that the police were unable to cope with a band of Mahomedans who were looting the bazaars, and asked permission to send two companies of an Indian regiment to restore order. I agreed. An hour later he asked for more troops and I authorized the use of the whole battalion. Later on he telephoned to say that the Indian troops were of no use, whereupon I gave orders for two companies of the Rifle Brigade to proceed to the scene of disturbance, and immediately after their arrival order was completely restored without a shot being fired.

Government House at Calcutta is a very large building, eminently suited for great receptions and parties, but a very uncomfortable house to live in, owing to the enormous distances of one wing from another. The living-rooms were in four separate blocks connected by long corridors with the reception-rooms in the centre of the house, and I remember that I had to walk over 250 yards on the same floor to reach my daughter's room from my own bedroom. The garden was very pretty with beds of cannas growing in great profusion, but was bounded on three sides by streets and on the fourth side by the *maidan* or park from which every night there was an inroad of jackals which made the night hideous with their cries. The trees also were full of flying foxes.

I was invited to become a member of the Calcutta Golf Club and on my first appearance was received by all the Committee and a large number of members to see me drive from the first tee. There was a big bunker about 120 yards off, which made my heart sink into my shoes when I saw it, but to my surprise and joy, and in spite of my nervousness, I carried it, and the Committee said that as far as golf was concerned I was a bit of " all right ", but they did not know what a poor performer I really was. This golf course proved an immense resource to me and provided me with the best form of exercise.

A few days later I rode out in the early morning with the Commander-in-Chief to visit the lines of the 8th Hussars and the Royal Artillery who had been brought into Calcutta to act as my escort on arrival. The grass on the *maidan* was slippery with very heavy dew, and as we cantered my horse slipped up sideways and fell with me on its side. The horse of the Commander-in-Chief reared at the same time and threw him to the ground. Neither of us was hurt, and I sat on the ground laughing so much that I could hardly get up. Nobody saw this incident except the members of our staffs, but if anybody had been handy with a Kodak he might have had an interesting picture of the Viceroy and the Commander-in-Chief laid out together.

A few days later I inspected also on the *maidan* a battalion of the West Kent Regiment which had also been brought to

12

Calcutta on the occasion of my arrival, and I had a pleasant surprise to find that the guard of honour drawn up at their camp was composed exclusively of men from Penshurst and the surrounding villages. I talked to each man individually and found I knew the families of some of them.

CHAPTER II

BENGAL AND OTHER
PROBLEMS, 1911

BEFORE I arrived in India I was well aware that the Province of Bengal was seething with sedition, the outcome of the policy of partition. Dacoities and assassinations of police and informers were almost of daily occurrence in Calcutta and its neighbourhood, and it was practically impossible to secure a conviction by the ordinary process of law. But I hardly realized till I was actually in Calcutta the state of political unrest and terrorism that prevailed, and the number of prosecutions for sedition that had been instituted and that were likely to extend over at least a year. Some of these prosecutions, in fact most of them, presented no likelihood of a successful issue and had been initiated through the shortsightedness of the Lieutenant-Governor, Sir Edward Baker, and his legal advisers. In India nothing could be worse than prosecutions that failed. They lowered the prestige of the Government and gave encouragement to the lawless. As soon as I had realized the true situation I sent for the Lieutenant-Governor and told him how much I disliked all these unsatisfactory prosecutions just at a moment when I was most anxious for a policy of conciliation in view of the impending visit of the King and Queen to India within a year's time; and I laid down the rule that no new political prosecution was to be initiated without my personal consent, and that in any pending case, where there was a doubt as to the sufficiency of evidence to secure a conviction, the prosecution was to be withdrawn. Sir E. Baker received his instructions with resignation, but I have seldom come across a greater fire-eater, and I always called him " my Bengal tiger ". The poor man was, however, ill at the time, though he did not know it, and he died within a year. It was only a few weeks later that I received a telegram from Lord Crewe, the Secretary of State, expressing his deep discontent with the administration of justice in Bengal and his wish that I should exercise supervision. I told Lord Crewe of the steps I had already taken, but I deprecated any open action in this sense which would have had a deleterious effect on other local governments where justice had been and was being well administered, and I promised to watch Bengal and to let the Lieutenant-Governor know that, in consequence of what had been going on in Bengal, the Secretary of State had proposed that no political prosecutions should be initiated without the approval of the Government of India. This I did, mentioning to Sir E. Baker Lord Crewe's dissatisfaction and that I had defended him in deprecating Crewe's proposal of supervision, but that I did not then know what his decision would be. The Bengal tiger was restive and uncomfortable, but his claws were cut.

During the following three months I succeeded, in consultation with Sir Lawrence Jenkins, Chief Justice of Bengal, in compromising the worst and most difficult prosecutions by inducing the accused to plead guilty on the understanding that they would be released but ordered to come up for sentence when required. These arrangements, unusual in themselves and justifiable only by the results they were intended to secure, were difficult to make owing to the tactlessness of the Advocate-General, while the animus of one of the Judges of the High Court against the executive made it difficult for the Civil Service to listen to any suggestion for a compromise. However, all prosecutions were completed or withdrawn before the arrival of their Majesties in India for the Durbar.

I had at this time a very curious Executive Council to deal with. The Commander-in-Chief, Sir O'Moore Creagh, had obtained the post as a *tertius gaudens* owing to Minto and Morley having rival candidates to fill Kitchener's vacancy and being unable to agree upon either. He had been a very gallant soldier of the Indian Army in his time, but he failed as an administrator. My Finance Member was Sir Guy Fleetwood Wilson, who was dependent upon the Secretary of the Finance Department, the late Lord Meston. The Home Member was Sir John Jenkins, a most able and useful man with whom I always got on extremely well and whose death and loss to me I deeply deplored a year later. Sir Robert Carlyle, Member of the Public Works Department, was the most difficult member of my Council. Sir William Clark was the Member for Commerce and Industry. He came out from England with me. A clever man, previously private secretary to Lloyd George. The Member for Education was Sir Harcourt Butler, a charming and able man, and a very good friend. He afterwards did useful work in the United Provinces to which I appointed him, and in Burma. Lastly, there was the Law Member, Sir Ali Imam, an Indian. There had been much doubt as to the advantage of having an Indian in the Viceroy's Executive Council; in fact, Lord Lansdowne had spoken to me of the fact in the most lugubrious and depreciatory terms, but I never experienced any disadvantage and he rendered me very useful service. I have a very happy remembrance of his invariable personal loyalty to me and of his exceptional usefulness. It was a strange team to handle, requiring a good deal of diplomacy, but I think I may say that we generally agreed in the end. I was defeated in Council only once and that was on the question of the creation of Indian Volunteer Corps during the war, and within a year of my departure from India these Corps were formed by my successor.

It was a month after my arrival in Calcutta that I held my first levee. From a spectacular point of view it was an interesting function. No less than 1,900 people attended it. I was so worn out after $1\frac{1}{2}$ hours' standing and bowing to each person as he passed that I nearly fainted and had to finish the levee sitting down. It was also very hot. I would suggest to anybody who is surprised at the above, to try what it is to make 1,900 bows standing and without stopping. The King never has more than 500 at a levee and seldom so many. I was greatly amused at receiving just before the levee the following letter. " Raja Pyari Mohun Mukerji regrets that the sudden aggravation of the pain in his legs caused by the proximity of the new moon prevents his attending the levee." I regard this as a real Indian gem.

I had to choose a Secretary to the Foreign Department and several candidates belonging to the Civil Service came and stayed with me so that I might select the one I considered most suitable. Although the Secretary to the Foreign Office is called the Foreign Secretary, he is not the real head of the Foreign Department, since from long custom the portfolio of that Department is always held by the Viceroy and the Foreign Secretary is to all intents and purposes what would be called an Under-Secretary in the Foreign Office in London. I had no need of an expert in foreign affairs, for from my service in the Foreign Office, I knew more about them than any other official in India. What I needed was an official who would cultivate and maintain friendly relations with the Ruling Princes and who would be a pleasant travelling companion when visiting Native States. Finally, I selected Sir H. MacMahon, Resident in Baluchistan, an agreeable personality. He was eventually appointed to succeed Kitchener in Egypt during the war.

Immediately after my arrival in Calcutta I commenced creating the necessary organization to carry out the Imperial Durbar which it was settled should be held towards the end of December 1911, the date being selected so as not to clash with religious festivals. I appointed a Committee under the Presidency of Sir John Hewett, Lieutenant-Governor of the United Provinces, to represent me, with other necessary officials and four Ruling Chiefs who were to be the other Members. Crewe begged me to keep the Committee well under my personal control, and this I did throughout through Colonel Maxwell, my Military Secretary, whom I appointed also to the Committee. I relieved Hewett of

17

his duties as Lieutenant-Governor and instructed him to proceed at once to Delhi in order to commence the preparation of the necessary plans. In the meantime I was in constant communication with Crewe and Stamfordham as to the procedure to be adopted and the ceremonial to be observed. One rather awkward incident occurred. It was decided that the King should bring his crown with him. Consequently everything was based on this assumption. But I was suddenly informed that the King's crown could not leave England and that the King proposed to order a special crown to be made. This was a bombshell as it was clearly intended that India should pay for it. In the meantime Sir Walter Lawrence came and stayed with me in Calcutta, and without consulting me suggested to the Maharajas of Burdwan and Tagore that subscriptions should be raised in British India and amongst the Ruling Chiefs to pay for the crown. This proposal pleased the people at home, but I vetoed it at once, as I felt that it would be highly derogatory to the position of the King to send round to collect money for His Majesty's crown. Supposing it failed ! I was very " fussed " over it all and finally placed the matter before my Council, who passed a resolution that to raise subscriptions for a crown in India would be politically disastrous, that the only course open was to pay for it from Indian revenues, and that after the Durbar it should be kept in London with the Imperial regalia. I insisted upon the latter point in spite of the views of Curzon, Stamfordham, Lawrence and others, that the crown might be kept at Delhi or in the Victoria Hall at Calcutta, for in my opinion the presence of a crown in India would present a real danger as an object of attainment in the event of a revolutionary upheaval, and a temporary victor would gain enormous prestige and authority were he able to obtain possession of the Royal Crown of India paid for by the Indian people. So the crown of India was ordered and paid for by the Government of India. This solved a question that had given much cause for thought, and proved generally satisfactory to so momentous an occasion.

During the early part of February the German Crown Prince visited India and I arranged all the details of his journey. He came accompanied by a large staff and to my regret without the Crown Princess, who is by far the best of that *ménage* in every way. I arranged shooting for him at various places, but he and his staff did not distinguish themselves. In the Sunderbunds they killed several water-buffaloes under the impression that they were wild buffaloes, but the Prince succeeded in getting a tiger in Jaipur, though curiously enough (as I heard later) the tiger travelled in a box in the same train as the Prince and roared so loudly during the night that he seriously disturbed the sleep of the travellers in the royal train. This was the Maharaja of Jaipur's own doing, and, as I was told, not the first time in similar circumstances.

The Prince came and stayed with me for about ten days at Government House, Calcutta, and I fêted him and did everything to make his visit a success. I gave him a great banquet, and in proposing his health I made an interesting statement that his family, i.e. the Hohenzollerns, was the only family of which I had known personally five generations, commencing with the Kaiser William I and ending with the Crown Prince's children.

On one occasion he behaved badly. He was staying with the Lieutenant-Governor of the United Provinces at Lucknow and suddenly disappeared. A great hunt was instituted by the police, who found him at Allahabad in the house of a pretty little Burmese princess of eminently good behaviour but much flattered by her success. Altogether he was a *bon enfant*, rather silly and effeminate. Every afternoon he and all his staff undressed and went to bed for three hours and it was a relief to be rid of them. When he left he gave me a pretty enamel and diamond cigarette-case, and the Kaiser sent me a glowing telegram of thanks and a very good portrait of himself in oils by Laszlo. I have never hung that picture anywhere, for I knew as an absolute certainty that there would be war with Germany and that his would be largely the responsibility. It has adorned my lumber room for fifteen years.

During all those winter months in Calcutta I presided regularly over the sittings of the Legislative Assembly, where the Viceroy acted as Prime Minister and Speaker. It was an arduous task, especially in the heat, for Calcutta became almost unbearably hot in the middle of February, so much so that I had to send Diamond up to Simla. The nights were stifling and mosquitoes innumerable. I had a very uncomfortable legacy from my predecessor in the Seditious Meetings Act which had to be passed and which met with almost universal condemnation. I allowed the members to blow off as much steam as they liked and finally I made a compromise that, although I would press for placing the Act on the Statute Book, the Act would only come into operation in proclaimed districts, and I said that it was for the people themselves in this way to render the Act abortive. This was readily accepted and the Bill passed unanimously. As a matter of fact, during the whole of the following five years of my Viceroyalty I never had occasion to proclaim a single district. Since the introduction of the Montagu-Chelmsford reforms an official Speaker to the Legislative Assembly is appointed by the Government, and the Viceroy no longer presides over the sittings of the Assembly. An official speaker would undoubtedly give more reasoned decisions on matters in dispute than would be the case with a Viceroy without great parliamentary experience and whose decision, whatever it might be, was final and indisputable ; but I cannot help feeling that under the reforms much of that good feeling and *bonhomie* which existed between the Viceroy and the members of the Legislative Assembly must have disappeared, while undoubtedly the proceedings were much more decorous in the presence of the Viceroy. I am well aware that on one or two occasions I gave mistaken decisions which I reversed later when shown privately that I had been wrong, but this only tended to make my relations with the Legislative Assembly more genial and friendly. I may add that during my administration every contentious measure, and some, such as the Indian " Dora ", were extremely drastic, were passed unanimously by the Assembly after my speech winding up the debate. Since the introduction of the so-called reforms, the sittings of the Assembly have become less orderly, while previously it had been a very dignified and sound legislative machine.

As an example of the extraordinary ignorance of ordinary Indians, I may mention an incident that occurred at the Howrah railway station on one occasion. I wished to present the King Edward medal to an Indian railway employee for having saved the lives of two children out of three at the risk of his own life. He was so terrified at the prospect that he had to be binged up with whisky beforehand. When he was brought up to me I was surprised to see him weeping piteously and holding his hands in a supplicating manner. I heard afterwards that he was frightened because he thought he was going to be punished for not having saved the life of the third child. When I pinned on his medal he was trembling with fear, but seemed more reassured when I said a few kind words to him. When he was cheered by the large crowds looking on he began to laugh and realized that nothing dreadful was going to happen to him.

My most friendly and delightful relations with Crewe as Secretary of State came to a temporary and abrupt ending in the beginning of March. He was dining with friends, mostly members of the Government, when after dinner he fell down unconscious as though he had had a stroke. It was due, they said, to overwork, the two posts of Secretary of State and Leader in the House of Lords being together beyond his strength. He was for several days in a very critical condition, but happily recovered his health entirely in a few months' time. In the meantime, Morley resumed his former position at the India Office, and I must say that it would be impossible to find an easier Secretary of State to deal with, though apparently this had not been the experience of my predecessor Lord Minto. They were, I think, politically irreconcilable. His very polished letters were

delightful reading and never contained a single word of dis-
agreement.

The four months that I had spent at Calcutta had been very
happy and full of interest. We had visitors with us all the time
and incessant functions of every kind. Still, it was all new and
everything went well. For recreation there was plenty of golf,
but I very soon found from experience that the early morning
ride on the racecourse, the general custom in Calcutta, was not
a good preparation for a hard day's work, while an evening ride
or game of golf was pleasant relaxation after a long day at the
desk.

Ex officio I was Chancellor of Calcutta University, and one
of my most interesting experiences was a surprise visit I paid at
7 a.m. one morning to the hostels and quarters inhabited by the
students. I was greatly shocked by the squalor and discomfort
of the students in the very insanitary dwellings in which they
lived. I was able to see everything as it really was, since I went
round all alone with a member of the Oxford Mission, and the
students had not the faintest idea who it was that was visiting
them. It only leaked out afterwards. As the result of my visit
I insisted with the Member for Education upon more funds
being applied to provide suitable hostels for the accommodation
of the 20,000 students in Calcutta, and before I left India I had
the satisfaction of seeing the Hardinge and other hostels opened.
I succeeded, however, in achieving a good deal more to secure
their greater comfort and prosperity in other ways.

On this and other occasions when I visited the University
hostels I was able to realize the futility of the education provided
for these Indian youths. I saw some of their notebooks containing long lectures on political economy and other subjects,
written in good handwriting, which they practically knew by
heart without understanding their meaning. These students
when questioned on their notes were quite unable to answer
satisfactorily for the simple reason that their knowledge of the
English language was inadequate to do so, but such was the craze

for English education that the newspapers were full of advertisements inserted by young men from the University offering themselves for appointments in which even " Failed B.A." was put forward as a minor recommendation and as a proof of having had a University education.

It was at this time that a certain Mr. Bose, a Bengali, asked if he might give a private lecture in Government House on the life of plants. I readily agreed, and he gave a most interesting lecture with magic lantern slides showing how the life of plants was affected by all or any of the vicissitudes that affect human life. He demonstrated by the most delicate instruments how plants sleep and wake, how they suffer pain, and how they react under the influence of drugs, etc. I discovered that his experiments were carried out by himself and volunteers at his own expense which he could ill afford, but I was so impressed by his exceptional scientific knowledge and by the wonderful experiments he had shown that I gave orders that provision should be made for a satisfactory laboratory to be prepared for him and every convenience to be placed at his disposal. He became the greatest scientist on plant life in the whole world, lectured all over Europe and the United States, and had a large building in Calcutta where his experiments are developed. He was also knighted.

As soon as the session of the Legislative Assembly in Calcutta was over I went to Delhi and spent a whole day from 8.30 a.m. to 7 p.m. with the Durbar Committee giving decisions on roads, Durbar arrangements, railways, polo grounds, camps, review ground, water-supply, lighting, drainage, etc. I was amused to see that, in spite of the great heat, I wore them all out by my energy and determination to see everything. There were already 20,000 people at work on the spot. It was a shock to me to find the interior of the Fort, where there was the Diwan-i-Am, Pearl Mosque and other incomparable buildings, littered with rubbish, bricks, stones, refuse, etc., and the Fort surrounded on one side by a wet marshy jungle on the river-bank, which I was told bred and harboured the most poisonous kind of mosquitoes. I at once gave orders that the whole of the interior of the Fort should be cleaned up and laid out as a garden with lawns, shrubs and water, and that the jungle outside the fort should be cut down, drained and turned into a park. This was done, and by the time of the Durbar, nine months later, the inside of the Fort was a lovely garden with flowering shrubs, fountains, lawns and runnels of fresh water, while the jungle outside had become a green park dotted with fine trees that had been concealed by overgrowth.

From Delhi I visited my grandfather's battlefields in the Punjab, in particular Moudkee and Feroshahur. At the latter place I had a great reception by the Sikhs, amongst them being three very old white-bearded veterans who had actually witnessed the battle as boys, one of them being able to give quite a good description of what he had seen. The 50th Battery of Artillery which had taken part in the battle was also present. The battle had been of a very critical nature owing to the very large number of Sikh guns and the very small and inadequate numbers of the British infantry. I held a Durbar and was presented with several old round shot and other trophies from the battlefield which I brought away with me.

I should mention here that in December 1910, almost immediately after my arrival in Calcutta, I heard of an old English gentleman, Mr. M. Power, 81 years old, and living in the town, who as a youngster of about 14 or 15 had actually accompanied a member of the staff of my grandfather, the Governor-General, to the first Sikh war, and had seen my grandfather, father and uncle frequently during that campaign and later at Simla. He was very feeble, but his mind was clear, and he gave me a very interesting account of much that he had seen. He presented me with a pamphlet in which he had described in a most graphic manner the battle of Moudkee with all its incidents and horrors.

At the conclusion of this visit I went to Lahore, where I stayed with the Lieutenant-Governor, Sir Louis Dane. I had an enthusiastic reception from the officials, Chiefs, and all classes who were interested in me as the grandson of the Governor-General who had annexed the Punjab and who had bestowed upon the Sikhs the peace, security and civilization which had hitherto been denied to them. During my stay I held a Durbar in Ranjit Singh's audience chamber, where my grandfather had actually signed Dhuleep Singh's deposition and the annexation of the Punjab. It was quite an historic occasion and a most picturesque sight with all the Chiefs and their Sirdars in brilliant robes and jewels, and brightly coloured tentings with palm-trees and water in the foreground. At the conclusion of the Durbar I led a procession on an enormous elephant covered with gold trappings, and followed by all the Chiefs on elephants through the native city of Lahore, where we were greeted with the greatest enthusiasm.

From Lahore I went to Quetta by the Bolan Pass and stayed with Colonel Archer, the Resident. It required four engines to pull our train up the pass and yet we could only do eight miles an hour ! I held a great Durbar in the Sandeman Hall, which was full of Baluchi Chiefs seated on the floor. The Chiefs, though wild looking, dirty and with long greasy hair protruding from under their turbans, were full of dignity and paid great attention to a long speech that I made to them. These Chiefs are some of the most loyal of the King's Indian subjects. I inspected the garrison and Staff College and on Sunday went to the Military Church in the cantonments. The singing of the choir was excellent, but none of the soldiers in the body of the church sang at all, simply because the General had made the mistake of issuing a general order that they should not sing on the occasion of the Viceroy's presence in Church ! I should have thought that a soldier would have foreseen such a result.

I was glad to have an opportunity of visiting the Staff College at Quetta commanded by General Braithwaite and to be present

25

at a very interesting field-day when, in spite of arrangements made in advance, a small skeleton force acting as the enemy completely defeated the General who was in command of the main force. The commander of the enemy was a very fat Colonel of the Essex Regiment who was very nearly kicked off at the march past afterwards.

When inspecting the various regiments at Quetta I was greatly impressed by the smartness and efficiency of a Hazara battalion commanded by a certain Major Jacob in the absence of the Colonel. I was told that unless he could obtain a staff appointment he would have to retire very shortly, and that his chances were small, as he was not on friendly terms with the Commander-in-Chief's Military Secretary. Anyhow, I insisted on a staff appointment being given to him, and he is now Field-Marshal Sir Claud Jacob, G.C.B. !

From Quetta I went to Chaman on the Afghan frontier, from which point one could look right across into Afghanistan towards Candahar. I there saw 73 miles of railway material collected in sheds for a rapid advance to Kandahar in case of need. Nothing had been omitted. There were even punches for the tickets. I admired greatly the courage of the wives of the British officers of the small garrison who lived in bungalows outside the fort and within about a mile of the frontier. They could have been raided by Afghan bandits any night.

On leaving Quetta for Karachi we passed through Sibi, where a number of Baluchi Chiefs had assembled to meet me. They had as a compliment roasted several sheep outside the station of which we had to select and eat a small portion in our fingers. My Indian servants had no scruples, for they devoured or carried off all that remained of the sheep.

I was favourably impressed by Karachi, a very go-ahead place with a promising future before it, but it is very ugly and with few architectural or other redeeming advantages. I opened there the " Hardinge Bridge " which had been built under the auspices of the Chairman of the Karachi Port Trust, Mr. Mules. I learnt privately that the bridge was appropriately called "Pons Asinorum"! but it was hoped I would not hear of this.

From Karachi to Dehra Dun we had to pass through the Sind Desert and Bahawalpur, where we were met by the Maharaja, a boy of 6, with his Ministers on the platform. The journey through the Sind Desert had been hot, but I have never felt such heat as when I got out of the train. It really knocked one down. I visited also the Sukkhur Bridge and irrigation works, a marvel of engineering skill. An unfortunate Indian regiment of cavalry was quartered there, the hottest place in India. The following day we reached Dehra Dun.

This was the close of my first official tour in India, lasting a fortnight in which I had covered four thousand miles, made twenty speeches and performed countless functions. It was a strenuous journey. At Dehra Dun I spent a peaceful fortnight before going to Simla for the summer. It is a beautiful and most delightful place at the foot of the Himalayas with snow-capped mountains only a few miles distant. I lived in a large bungalow in a lovely garden with no other buildings anywhere near. We were under the protection of several Ghurka battalions, whose headquarters were there. There was a good golf course and a further attraction was that we were only five or six miles distant from some excellent jungles full of game of various kinds. On this occasion we went into camp in the jungle for a week and killed three big tigers and a number of stags. Dehra Dun is the place that I liked best in India, and of which I have the happiest memories.

From Dehra Dun we went to Simla in the first week of May. I looked forward to going there with great interest as the name was so familiar to me from my earliest childhood owing to a reproduction of a Hindu temple at Simla built by my father in the woods at South Park. We went by motor-car, a tedious but picturesque journey mounting by winding roads from the plain at the edge of steep precipices through lovely mountain scenery to a height of 8,000 feet. We had the usual official reception and I was greatly pleased with my first impressions of Viceregal Lodge and grounds which were only strengthened by time.

The house was indeed very comfortable and just like an English country house with fine reception rooms. During my stay in India I added to the house a large room for the Legislative Assembly and some additional bedrooms of which there was a shortage. The gardens and views were lovely, especially the rose garden and herbaceous border. For these I give full credit to Lady Minto, who had planned them all.

Simla is an extraordinary place built on a hogback ridge with bungalows on the sloping sides. There was only one main road along the ridge and on this road were collected all the Government buildings, the church, hotels, shops, schools, etc. The officials inhabited very comfortable houses on the slopes. Locomotion was very restricted and no motor-cars or carriages were allowed except for the Viceroy, Commander-in-Chief and the Governor of the Punjab. The rest of the Simla world went in rickshaws. It was a gay place in the summer months as so many people came up from the plains to avoid the hot weather. There was a great deal of tennis, polo and other matches at Annandale, but at the same time it was a place of hard work in the Government offices, and I do not think the Government of India would be able to carry on unless they were able to go to Simla or elsewhere for the hot weather.

A charming week-end resort is also allotted to the Viceroy at Mashobra, seven miles distant and 1,000 feet higher than Simla, on the road to Thibet from which the most glorious views of the snow ranges of the Himalayas can be seen. I was very fond of this place with its peace and quiet.

On my way from Dehra Dun to Simla I paid another visit to Delhi and was very pleased to find that during the month that had elapsed since my last visit great progress had been made and that the Durbar preparations were being pressed forward with feverish activity. One of the most interesting sights was that of hundreds of native gardeners sitting on their hams in long serried lines sowing blades of grass to make out of waste land polo grounds and lawns, all of which were glorious green lawns by the end of the rains.

It may well be imagined how difficult it was to come to an agreement with the Court and India Office authorities upon the ceremonial and other arrangements for a great Durbar, apart from all those that had to be made for the presence of the Ruling Chiefs of India, about 200 in number, the Provincial Governments, 70,000 or 80,000 troops, and a large number of foreigners and sightseers, all of whom would have to be brought to the camps, lodged and fed, practically doubling the population of Delhi (which was 250,000) for the space of about a fortnight. But what made things infinitely more difficult was the presence in England of certain persons who had been in India, and who kept on offering suggestions to the King and the Court, most of which were quite unpractical, and who criticized the proposals we put forward. The result was repeated changes of plans which became intolerable, and I had finally to point out that in view of the imminence of the rains when work would have to be suspended, any further changes would be out of the question. Their pertinacity was exasperating, and finally I conveyed to the King that while I was being incessantly bothered with paltry details, 233 camps covering 25 square miles and with 10 square miles of canvas had been laid out; 40 miles of new roads were under construction in addition to 20 miles of roads in the military camps; 26½ miles of broad-gauge and 9 miles of narrow-gauge railway with 24 new railway stations were being built ; 50 miles of water mains were being supplied, and 30 miles of waterpipes for the distribution of water in the camps. Electric light was being provided in sufficient amount to light two fair-sized towns such as Portsmouth and Brighton. Farms were being established with herds of milch cows and dairies and markets for the supply of meat, vegetables, etc. All these activities were being carried out in addition to the preparation of the actual Durbar amphitheatre, the construction of review grounds, polo grounds, football grounds and other necessary works. After my letter containing these details had reached London I had no more trouble, for it was realized that the task I had in hand was far more gigantic than they had ever been able to realize, and that any advice they could give was futile and superfluous. Of course there were details of ceremonial, etc., that were under discussion to the very end, but there was no more interference from home in the general scheme and plans for the holding of the Durbar.

CHAPTER III

THE ARMY: INDIAN STATES:
DURBAR PREPARATIONS, 1911

IT was soon after my arrival in India that the question of reduction in the military expenditure was raised in the Legislative Assembly, a proposition to which my Council had already agreed in principle in view of the imminent loss of four millions sterling of opium revenue from a total of just over 50 millions, and on which subject the Commander-in-Chief had promised to make definite proposals within six months. The military situation in India had entirely changed owing to the conclusion of our agreement with Russia in 1907, which excluded Russia as our potential enemy on the Indian frontier, leaving only Afghanistan and China as possible enemies, the former not being regarded as a first-class military power, and the other being to a certain extent negligible owing to the inaccessibility of the Anglo-Chinese frontier. It was my desire and intention not to reduce the fighting material of the Indian Army but to abolish or reduce some of those military units that were practically useless for fighting or even peace-preserving purposes. This was brought home to me by the presence in Calcutta of a native regiment that I really regarded as *opéra-bouffe* soldiers. Looking from my window one day I saw a sentry from this regiment at the gate of Government House smoking a cigarette with his shoes off and his rifle resting against the gate! General Willcocks, in command of the troops in Bengal, came to inspect this regiment and told them that they were the worst regiment he had ever seen anywhere. I refused after this to have them on guard at Government House. And yet this worthless regiment cost as much as a good fighting regiment and there were others like it. Consequently I wrote an official memorandum on the subject explaining my views and pointing out where economies and reductions might be made without affecting the fighting strength of the army. This memorandum provoked a very long memorandum by the Chief of the General Staff (General Haig) and the Army Department in which they fought hard against any reductions whatever, even of those regiments which they regarded as worthless, and on which they advocated additional expenditure. To cut a long story short, the memorandum on the needs of the Army in India drawn up by the General Staff was of a most secret nature and was intended for my consideration and that of my Council only. Happily I regarded it as so secret that I gave permission for only about twenty copies to be printed containing my memorandum and the reply of the General Staff, and insisted that they should all be numbered and a list kept of the persons to whom they were distributed. Information reached me later from London that there had been a leakage somewhere and that articles based on garbled accounts had appeared in *The Times* and *Standard*. I heard also privately that a copy had been sent to the War Office in London. I sent for the Commander-in-Chief and accused the Army Department of having sent home a copy. As he denied this I ordered him to call in all the copies that had been issued, and when this was done the missing copy was found to be that of a general of the General Staff who admitted that he had sent his copy to the War Office. The Commander-in-Chief expressed to me his anger and annoyance at this incident, but as General Creagh seemed quite unable to handle the matter and asked me to do so, I felt it my duty to point out to the general his very flagrant and serious breach of trust, and I reproached him for his inexcusable behaviour. He had not a word to say in his defence.

This, however, was not my only trouble with the General Staff, for in October 1911 I was secretly informed that correspondence was in progress between the War Office in London and the General Staff in India as to the number of divisions that could be sent to Europe from India in the event of a continental crisis.

In India there were, in addition to other troops, six complete divisions maintained at war strength. The General Staff agreed to supply three, and with difficulty four of these divisions. Now I was not opposed to the idea of the despatch of Indian divisions to Europe in the event of war, for as will be shown later I was responsible for the initiative in sending Indian divisions in 1914 to the scene of action in France in the Great War. But I resented that a discussion of this nature should be carried on between the War Office and the General Staff in India without my knowledge or the knowledge of the Government of India, and, as it proved, without the knowledge of the India Office or of the Secretary of State. Crewe was very much upset when he received this news and he talked the matter over with the Prime Minister, Haldane and Grey. In view of later events it is of interest to record what Crewe wrote in reply : "Now not only have the Cabinet never given assent to Indian troops being thus employed,[1] but I do not believe that they would ever agree to such a use. This is Asquith's opinion as well as mine, and also that of Grey, who was there when we talked over this part of the subject. Asquith said he would never, in any circumstances, agree to such a use of Indian troops." Three years later, on the outbreak of war, two infantry and two cavalry divisions were sent to France from India in the early months of the war, the same Prime Minister and the same Government being in office in London !

It was in May that the news was received of the murder of a political officer, Williamson by name, by a tribe called Abors on the frontier of Eastern Bengal. He had crossed the frontier and penetrated into their country without permission. Nevertheless, it was impossible to tolerate his treacherous murder and a small punitive expedition was sent into the Abor country, which returned as soon as chastisement in the form of destruction of villages had been completed.

About this time the Maharaja of Jodhpur unluckily died.

[1] In Europe.

His death was a loss, as he was a good ruler of sterling loyalty. The question then arose as to the Regency during the minority of the young Maharaja. His uncle the Maharaja of Idar, General Sir Pertab Singh, was very anxious to become Regent, and it would have been impossible to find a better Regent, but the Agent to the Governor-General in Rajputana was opposed to the idea, as also the Political Department in Simla. Nevertheless, in view of Sir Pertab's well-known loyalty and devotion to the British Raj as well as his exceptionally high and chivalrous character combined with his fondness for his nephew, I over-ruled all such objections and appointed him Regent. I never had cause to regret this decision.

This was an example of those cases where the Foreign Department almost invariably endeavoured to obtain the control of the State through the Resident during the minority of the Prince, a system to which, except in certain special cases, I took serious objection, since it met with general disapproval by Indians in the States.

As an Indian Sir Pertab was a very great man. His courage was extraordinary and he did not know what fear meant. He excelled as the best pig-sticker in India, but he had been trained to fight a boar on foot with only a knife in his hand, and when the boar charged he would jump aside, catch the boar by a hind leg as it passed and kill it with one blow of the knife. He was of Spartan simplicity, and I myself have seen the box in which he slept as a youth till the age of 21. Although of short stature, the box was too short for him to stretch out at full length. His influence amongst the young men of Jodhpur was admirable, and Jodhpur became under his influence the centre of chivalry and sport in India. He was truly " a white man " among Indians. I shall never forget seeing Sir Pertab after receiving from the King the order of the G.C.B. at the end of the Great War, where he had served with distinction at the front, sitting in the entrance to the Alexandra Hotel with the insignia beside him in a state of blissful satisfaction, so that all could see it, and receiving congratulations from everybody who came into the hotel at receiving an honour never before bestowed upon an Indian.

The engagement of Scindia, Maharaja of Gwalior, to the daughter of the Maharaja of Baroda was announced in the summer of 1911. I was not very happy about it as I had a great respect and affection for Scindia, who became one of my greatest friends in India, while Baroda was at that time said to be of very doubtful loyalty and his Maharani was credited with being in close communication with Madame Cama, a well-known Indian revolutionary in Europe. The news of the breaking off of the engagement a few months later was a great relief, though Scindia never saw again the £20,000 worth of jewellery that he had given his fiancée. She married later a son of the Maharaja of Cooch Behar, who, however, died soon afterwards. Scindia was simply devoted to his first wife, a charming little lady, but she had no children. She and he therefore agreed that it was necessary he should marry a second wife. A few months later he came to announce to me his engagement to a second wife, and he did a very unusual thing in showing me a photograph of his fiancée. Of course I said that she was very beautiful. She bore him two children, a daughter to whom I am godfather, and later a son, to whom the King was godfather, so that the succession to the state was secured. I was amused to learn that after the birth of these children they were placed under the charge of the Maharaja's mother and of the first wife, the second wife and real mother having little to say as regards their care and upbringing.

A piece of luck for me happened in the application by Sir Edward Baker, Lieutenant-Governor of Bengal, for four months' leave of absence with the possible intention of retiring at its close. Much as I liked him personally I found him quite hopeless as Lieutenant-Governor of such a difficult province as Bengal. He recommended as his successor Mr. Slacke, the Senior Member of his Council, but as I had had experience of him in connection with the Hatwa Estate I refused to agree and appointed Sir William Duke as Acting Lieutenant-Governor. Sir E. Baker never returned to India and died soon after the expiration of his leave. Sir W. Duke justified entirely his appointment.

The moment has now arrived to give an account of the most important decision that I took during the $5\frac{1}{2}$ years of my Vice-royalty, and which pervaded the whole of that period.

It was in the month of January 1911, barely two months after my arrival in India, that I received a proposal from Lord Crewe suggesting the possibility of a modification of the partition of Bengal, which had been effected by Lord Curzon, and which had ever since been a festering political sore and the cause of all the anarchical agitation in Bengal. His proposal was intended to satisfy that section of the Indian political community who regarded the partition as a mistake. His idea was to create a Governorship instead of a Lieutenant-Governorship of Bengal with the capital of the Province at Dacca or elsewhere, to form an Imperial Enclave of Calcutta directly under the Viceroy, and to appoint Commissioners for various divisions, as in Sind. The suggestion was that the rectification of the partition should be announced by the King at the Durbar, His Majesty being strongly in favour of it in principle. Before replying to this proposal I consulted several officials in responsible positions, since having been hardly two months in the country I was not in a position to give a definite opinion of my own, and as all those whom I consulted pointed out very strong objections to it, I declared the scheme to be impracticable, and Crewe thereupon allowed it to drop.

During later months it was brought home to me that if there was to be peace in the two Bengals it was absolutely necessary to do something to remove what was regarded by all Bengalis as an act of flagrant injustice without justification. There was at the same time a feeling of expectancy abroad that something would be done at the time of the Durbar to remove this injustice, and I appreciated the fact that if nothing were done we would have to be prepared for even more serious trouble in the future than in the past in Bengal. Moreover, I realized after six months in Calcutta that the Government of Bengal was practically non-existent as far as the maintenance of peace and order was concerned, that it was really the Viceroy who administered the Province and that it was to him and his Council that the Lieutenant-Governor and his officials looked for advice and support. Moreover, the presence of the Legislative Assembly in Calcutta created an undue and inevitable Bengali influence upon the Members, which was detrimental to their legislative impartiality and presented a field for intrigue in which the Bengalis excelled. All these aspects of the situation in Bengal were most unsatisfactory and were a constant source of anxiety to me, for which I did not then see the remedy. It was Sir John Jenkins, the Home Member of my Council, who in a letter to me dated the 17th June 1911 sent me a memorandum which caused my views to materialize into a definite policy. He, as the Member responsible for security in India, held very strong views upon the urgency of the transfer of the Capital from Calcutta to Delhi which he thought " would be a bold stroke of statesmanship which would give universal satisfaction and mark a new era in the history of India ". With this scheme the reversal of the partition of Bengal was to be associated as well as other changes in the delimitation of the provinces. He urged that these changes should be announced by the King in Durbar at Delhi, and he expressed his opinion that the change would be magical since, in the imagination of the masses of the people, Delhi and Empire have been associated from time immemorial. What Sir John did not fully appreciate was the implacable opposition that would be offered to the scheme by the British commercial community in Calcutta, who resented the change of Calcutta from an Imperial to a Provincial capital, and the loss of prestige due to the withdrawal of the Viceroy, Commander-in-Chief, Government of India, Legislative Assembly and a host

37

of officials to a new capital at Delhi. Otherwise Sir John Jenkins' forecast proved absolutely correct.

It is as well that I should mention here that the idea of removing the capital from Calcutta to Delhi was not entirely original since Lord Lawrence had considered the scheme and was in favour of it, but did not succeed in overcoming the opposition of his Council. I was informed by Sir Valentine Chirol that Lord Curzon had also considered the removal of the capital to Agra, but admitted to him that he had not the courage to press it.

After long discussion with Sir J. Jenkins, with whose views I was quickly in general agreement, I drew up a very secret memorandum which I submitted to the Members of my Council for their opinion. The principal points were : (1) The transfer of the capital from Calcutta to Delhi. (2) The creation of United Bengal into a presidency with a Governor in Council appointed from England. (3) The creation of Behar and Orissa into a Lieutenant-Governorship with a Legislative Council and a capital at Patna, and (4) the restoration of the Chief Commissionership of Assam. All the members of my Council agreed in principle, some of them pointing out objections that might be raised to the scheme, none of which were however in any way vital. I decided therefore to submit the scheme for the consideration of the Secretary of State, giving him not only my own views but those of all and each of the members of my Council. On the 19th July I wrote a long letter to Crewe containing full details of the policy I proposed, placing before him the advantages to be obtained, and the objections that might be raised, but advocating strongly its acceptance as the best and only certain means of securing peace and reconciliation in Bengal, with at the same time a statesmanlike change in the general situation of the Government of India. I urged upon Crewe the necessity for extreme secrecy whether my scheme was accepted or not, and I told him that I felt this need so strongly that I myself made copies of all my letters on the subject, while the notes of the Members of my Council had been privately typewritten.

It was on the 7th August that I received a very satisfactory telegram from Crewe telling me that I had his " entire support and full authority to proceed ". He agreed that the first announcements as regards Delhi and the Governorship of Bengal must be made at the Durbar and that absolute secrecy should be maintained till then. He asked at the same time that he should receive a formal despatch from my Government which I could send to him personally as a private letter for the sake of secrecy, and which should be prepared with a view to ultimate publication in its entirety.

I had already drafted an official despatch to Crewe setting forth my scheme in elaborate detail. When I understood that it was to be for ultimate publication I revised it, and after certain modifications suggested by Members of my Council, it assumed the form in which it was eventually published as a State paper. It became later the subject of acute controversy in the House of Lords, although history has since entirely vindicated its conclusions.

Lord Crewe confided the substance of my scheme in the first instance to the King in the presence of Sir A. Bigge.[1] H.M. accepted it with great keenness, was very anxious to make the announcement himself at the Durbar, and was very insistent as to the need of complete secrecy. Later Crewe confided it to Lord Morley and Asquith. Both were deeply impressed and favourable, being struck by the adroitness with which the creation of new grievances was avoided while removing old ones. Asquith was greatly struck by the bigness of the idea and considered that its merits and advantages far outweighed any hostile arguments, though he anticipated, like many others, much opposition and grumbling from the Calcutta Europeans. As far as this question was concerned the remaining months before the Durbar were fully occupied in considering the legislative and statutory measures that would be necessary to carry out the new policy, all of which had to be done with the greatest care so as

---

[1] Afterwards Lord Stamfordham.

to ensure secrecy. The secret was known to only twelve people in India during the six months that preceded the Durbar on December 11 and there was absolutely no leakage at all. On November 3rd I was informed by Crewe that the India Council in London was in favour of the scheme, and it was accepted a few days later by the Cabinet.

While this great and important scheme was under discussion I was still very fully occupied with administrative questions such as a comprehensive education policy, reduction of expenditure rendered necessary by the loss of four millions from opium revenue and the general Government of the country, while preparations for the Durbar were being feverishly pushed forward, and many questions such as the temporary increase of honours for distribution by the King, the striking of Durbar medals, the programme of the Durbar, the preparation of the camps, and the transport of visitors from the Provinces and of Ruling Chiefs with their suites, presented endless problems requiring careful thought, tactful handling and rapid action. As an example, one ruling Chief announced his intention of bringing with him two tame tigers with his camp ! I had to protest and finally to forbid the arrival of these tigers, pointing out to the Chief that, however tame they might be, they could not fail to be a source of alarm in the neighbouring camps and of disturbance when they howled at night.

A question that preoccupied me greatly was that of the King's charger and carriage horses. Knowing how difficult it was to find a really fine charger for the King that would be quiet and well trained, I urged upon H.M. to bring out two or three chargers with him, but he declined to do so and appointed Colonel Grimston of the Indian Army to find him in India a charger and the necessary horses for the State carriages which the King was to use. I had offered my State carriage horses, which were most beautiful horses and thoroughly trained for State functions, but they were declined. I do not know why. Anyhow, a charger was eventually bought from General Woon, a small dark brown horse, very quiet but of no appearance. It compared very un-favourably with my charger, a coal-black English thoroughbred, standing seventeen hands, which had formerly belonged to an officer in the Blues. I would have offered it to the King but it was not sufficiently quiet, as the King admitted when he saw my horse dancing at the big review ! So also with the carriage horses. I had laid down that the King and Queen were to arrive in a State carriage with six horses while my carriage was to have four. I arrived at the Durbar in advance of Their Majesties so as to receive them, my four very high-stepping horses with outriders being the admiration of everybody, and my disgust may be imagined when I saw later the King and Queen arrive with only four horses to their carriage, and not worthy specimens at that. I expostulated with Colonel Grimston later, and his excuse was that the two leaders had gone sick, but I would not accept that excuse as I still had twenty more carriage horses in my stable that were available. It was a stupid case of personal pride on the part of Grimston, who did not like to admit that he had failed and had to borrow from me horses for the King. However, when the King and Queen came to Calcutta as my guests I insisted that only my own horses would be used in the State carriages.

It was in August 1911 that the Nizam of Hyderabad died from alcoholic poisoning. He was a loss as he had always been loyal and his State well governed. It is extraordinary how many Ruling Chiefs are apt to die from excessive drink. There are doubtless many reasons for this : possibly the climate and their mode of life play their part. My belief is that these excesses are due to the number of their wives. He was succeeded by his son and I decided to pay without delay a visit to the young Nizam at Hyderabad. It was a long and hot journey by train of three days and nights each way, but it was worth it as I secured the confidence and trust of the Nizam who, during the whole time I was in India, acted in a most exemplary manner. I stayed with him twice at Hyderabad and he visited me twice at Simla. He wanted on one occasion to bring fifteen wives with him to Simla, but I protested and they were left in camp at the foot of the hills. In those days he was on very close terms of friendship with me, and never took any step in his State without first asking my advice.

Hyderabad is a curious place, with no fine buildings or palaces and nothing stately in any way, but it is situated in the midst of a very rich and prosperous country. Although the population is principally Hindu the ruling classes are Moslems and the Nizam's troops are a motley collection of Arabs, negroes, Portuguese and others.

In October I paid a further visit to Delhi after four months' absence in order to ascertain the progress of the preparations for the Durbar. The change was quite miraculous. Where there had been fields of waving corn in May there was a large railway station with ten platforms, each 300 yards long, and capable of coping with any amount of railway traffic. There were two splendid polo grounds with three pavilions and sunk gardens with terraces in the most perfect order where there had been nothing but cultivation before. The King's camp, covering 85 acres, was beautifully laid out with red roads, green lawns and rose gardens with roses from England. The fort at Delhi which had been a wilderness was sparkling with fountains, water runnels, green lawns and shrubberies, while the scene of the forthcoming Durbar was gradually assuming its final form with magnificent and stately pavilions and seating accommodation for 100,000 people, and space for 30,000 troops. Everything else was on the same scale.

The last four months before the arrival of the King and Queen for the Durbar were months of ceaseless activity and it was then only that I loosed the pursestrings and began disbursing freely the million pounds entrusted to my care for running the Durbar. It may not be out of place to state here that after the Durbar and State visit to Calcutta had been completed and the value of the tents and other equipment realized by sales, the total cost of

THE VICEROY'S DURBAR AT CHOWMAHALLA PALACE, HYDERABAD

the Durbar and the Imperial visit to India amounted to only £660,000, while many of the permanent constructions such as roads, railway sidings, etc., made for the Durbar, remained of public utility.

CHAPTER IV

THE KING'S DURBAR, 1911-1912

THE King left England in H.M.S. *Medina* on November 9th.

Before I left Delhi to meet the King and Queen at Bombay it was decided to have dress rehearsals of all the most important ceremonies. I had time to attend only one of them, viz. the Durbar ceremony, and it was a complete fiasco. I was very disappointed and seriously alarmed lest all the other ceremonies should be the same, and I was told after my return from Bombay that the other dress rehearsals had all been equally bad. Yet, strange to say, when the real ceremonies took place, not the slightest hitch occurred, and they were all absolutely perfect.

On the 1st December I left for Bombay and stayed two days before the King's arrival with Sir George Clarke, the Governor, in order to superintend the landing and other arrangements. On the day before the expected arrival of Their Majesties I received a wireless message that I was to come on board the *Medina* at ten o'clock next morning with the Naval Commander-in-Chief in full uniform, but that I was not to fly the Viceroy's flag on my launch nor was any salute to be fired when I embarked. I carried out my instructions to the letter, and as I passed the ships of the Royal Indian Marine they all "manned ship", while when I passed the King's escort of cruisers one could see the bluejackets swabbing decks, etc. On arrival alongside the *Medina* the Commander-in-Chief and I were received by a bluejacket, while Admiral Keppel received me in undress uniform, in spite of the fact that it was he who had transmitted to me the wireless message that the Naval Commander-in-Chief, his superior officer, and I were to come in full uniform. The

King's suite were lounging about the deck in flannels, etc. Sir Edmund Slade, the Admiral, was simply rabid at this treatment, and as we climbed the ladder said he was going to speak to Admiral Keppel who was in command of the *Medina*, but I absolutely forbade him to say a word to anybody. I was very curt with Admiral Keppel and insisted on being taken immediately to the King's suite of cabins.

I was received by H.M. in full naval white uniform and by the Queen, who both greeted me with the greatest warmth, and they insisted on my remaining with them until four o'clock in the afternoon discussing plans, receiving and presenting the Governor of Bombay and other official visitors. A remarkable testimony to the discretion of the King was that when I began to speak of the transfer of the Capital from Calcutta to Delhi the Queen expressed her surprise and asked what it all meant. H.M. had considered the matter so secret that he had not even mentioned it to the Queen! I imagine that there are very few people who under similar circumstances would have displayed equal discretion.

In the evening the King gave a large dinner on board the *Medina* to which I was also invited. As an example of the ignorance of the King's suite as to etiquette under similar conditions I was told, rather brusquely by the Equerry in Waiting, though I arrived at exactly the hour at which I had been invited, that I was the last to arrive. I had to explain to him that, though no longer Viceroy since the arrival of the King, I was still Governor-General of India, and that it was my duty to arrive last since any person arriving after me would be wanting in respect and politeness to me and indirectly to the King. I really believe that the King's suite were under the impression that I had no position in India after the arrival of the King! They soon learnt otherwise.

On the following day the King and Queen made their official landing at Bombay, which was carried out with great pomp and splendour, and drove through parts of the town where

45

they received a very enthusiastic welcome. They returned on board ship and I asked permission, which was accorded, to return at once to Delhi so that I might supervise the very last preparations for their reception.

Their Majesties arrived on the morning of the 7th December in the Imperial train, which was the Viceroy's usual train, at Salimgarh station inside the Fort at Delhi, and was received there by myself and my wife, the Governors, Lieutenant-Governors and Members of my Council, and after presentation of all the Indian Ruling Chiefs assembled in a large tent close to the station a procession was formed for the State Entry into Delhi. Just before mounting our horses Stamfordham saw my beautiful black thoroughbred charger standing alongside the King's horse, and asked me whose it was. When I said it was mine he asked me why I had not lent it to the King to ride, to which I replied that I knew from experience that H.M. would find the horse at times a handful and difficult to ride. As a rule he behaved splendidly, but at reviews he became excited and liked to show himself off. At the big review at Delhi when the King and I had to canter across the parade ground he became so excited that the King remarked to me how glad he was not to be riding my horse.

I had tried to persuade the King to ride an elephant at the State Entry which would have been the correct thing and a distinguishing mark, but he had always flatly refused. In order therefore that there should be no doubt as to which was the King, I had given orders that those in front should always keep 50 yards ahead of H.M., while I, riding with Crewe, kept 50 yards behind him. As we passed through the densely crowded streets I noticed that the people did not recognize the King, who after all was a small man, was dressed in a red coat like other Generals and was riding a small horse. He also did not make any kind of demonstration to the people. At the same time as I passed along the people cheered and I could hear them say, " There is the Lord Sahib, but where is the King ? " I there-

fore rode up to the King and suggested to him that he should
salaam to the people since by that alone they would recognize
that it was he who was the King. H.M. told me at the time
that he was disappointed at his non-recognition by the people.
Otherwise the State Entry was a huge success and everything
went off quite perfectly. The procession lasted for hours since
after that of Their Majesties there was a procession of all the
Ruling Princes and Chiefs with their suites and retainers in every
kind of costume, both modern and mediæval, which was, I was
told, most entertaining for those who could watch it.

In view of events at Delhi a year later I would mention here
the precautionary measures taken to secure the safety of the
King and Queen during their stay. Delhi is a town of mixed
population and has been the scene of murder reprisals from
endless times before and during Moghul rule. So anxious was
I that there should be no untoward incident that I personally
supervised and assumed full responsibility for all measures taken.
In the first place I ascertained that there were over 300 dangerous
characters in Delhi, so I gave orders that on the day before the
King's arrival they should be arrested and lodged in prison
until after the King had left Delhi. In the meantime they were
to be made as comfortable as possible and well treated and fed.
This was done and similar measures were later taken before the
King went to Calcutta. Nobody complained, not a word of
criticism appeared in the press, and the general Indian public
considered that it was quite the right step for a strong Government to have taken. These steps did not, however, suffice.
The danger spot in my opinion was the Chandni Chowk, the
main street of Delhi, where on one side the procession would
have to pass almost under the windows of the houses. In this
street I allowed nobody to stand on the pavement except the
British regiments lining the street : I brought up 4,000 police
from the neighbouring provinces and had a police officer at
every window and allowed nobody on the roofs of the houses.
The backs of the houses were guarded by Indian troops and

nobody was allowed in or out of any of the houses after 6 a.m., though the procession was to pass only at 11 a.m. During those five hours the police had to search the houses and see that they harboured no bad characters. All these instructions were carried out, but nevertheless I breathed a sigh of relief when we had safely reached the end of the street. It was there that I was bombed a year later.

The King and Queen were extremely pleased with their own camp and its surroundings and I am sure that no tents in any camp have ever been more luxurious and comfortable. My own camp and the camps of the various provincial Governors, Ruling Chiefs, military and visitors' camps, etc., covered a space of no less than 20 square miles, and at night looking down from the ridge one could see the plain sparkling with electric light almost as far as the eye could see. It was a marvellous sight and there were no less than a quarter of a million people living under canvas who had to be fed and provided with all the necessaries of life for which the resources of the City of Delhi were quite inadequate since its population was also only a quarter of a million. To meet this demand I had seen that market gardens, herds of cows and dairies, bakeries, butcher shops and all that was needed to feed a quarter of a million people for a fortnight was in readiness, but the sanitary question was the most difficult and also dangerous with such a mixed crowd coming from all parts of India with the possibility of their bringing with them plague, cholera or other infectious ailments. Thanks to the strenuous efforts of the Indian Medical Service, this danger was entirely averted and there was no sickness during the whole period of the occupation of the camp.

As soon as Their Majesties were settled down they received visits from all the Chiefs and, as the King asked me to return for him the visits of all those who had the right to a return visit, I had no less than seventy visits to return in State. This I did for several mornings, commencing at 9 a.m., staying only five minutes in each camp. The only incident that occurred

THE KING-EMPEROR AND LORD HARDINGE ON THE WAY TO THE
PROCLAMATION PARADE, DELHI

was when I visited the Maharaja of Bhutan. My arrival was announced by six Bhutanese trumpeters with trumpets about 20 feet long, each trumpet being supported on the shoulders of two men. They gave such fearful and hideous blasts that the horses of my State carriage, usually the quietest possible, were simply terrified and became unmanageable. Nevertheless, the Bhutanese still continued blowing hard from very powerful lungs until one of my A.D.C.s went and stopped them. It amused me greatly, but I would not allow the performance to be repeated when I left.

There was one other incident which might have been of consequence if I had not detected the intrigue. When returning, on behalf of the King, the visit of the Maharaja of Kashmir, I remarked on the absence from the Durbar of the Maharaja's heir, Hari Singh, the present Maharaja, and I asked where he was. The Maharaja replied in a tone so that everybody could hear what he said, "That is my heir", and pointed to a little boy who proved to be the son of the Maharaja of Poonch. I remarked, "I do not know him", and promptly left the Durbar. When outside the Durbar tent I sent the Foreign Secretary back to the Maharaja to ask what he had meant by announcing in open Durbar that the son of the Maharaja of Poonch was his heir, and to say that I would not admit it. Had I not objected there is little doubt that the real heir would have been deposed from his position, but in excuse of his action the Maharaja explained to the Foreign Secretary that the boy was only his "spiritual heir", whatever that might mean. He was a sly old fox.

The secret of the transfer of the capital to Delhi, though known in India to twelve people and to about the same number of people in England, had been singularly well kept for a period of six months, not a whisper of what was impending having been heard. I imagine it was one of the best-kept secrets in history. The difficulty was how to maintain this secrecy until the King made the announcement at the Durbar and at the same time to prepare and print the requisite gazettes, news-sheets, fly-leaves, etc. After much thought I decided to form a separate camp which I called the Press Camp and to instal there printing machines with living accommodation for all the secretaries, printers, etc., and their servants, who would be required for this purpose and to provision it for three days. Having collected the necessary staff, they were all put into this " Mystery Camp " three days before the Durbar and a cordon of troops and police placed round the camp so that nothing could go in or out until the actual moment of the Durbar. This proved a complete success, and as the copies of the announcements were all placed in sealed envelopes and only distributed in the Durbar after the King's Speech had been delivered, complete secrecy was maintained and the effect was even a greater surprise than could have been anticipated six months earlier.

I do not propose to give here a full description of the many great and historic ceremonies that took place during the presence of Their Majesties at Delhi, but I shall limit my efforts to reminiscences of the more interesting incidents that occurred.

The day on which the Durbar was held was a perfect winter's day with a bright sun, blue sky and cool breeze. It was a piece of good fortune as 30 miles away there was a deluge of rain. As I drove up in State to the Durbar before the arrival of Their Majesties whom it was my duty to receive, the spectacle was really as magnificent as it was possible to imagine, but typical of Indian methods, the last few nails were being driven into the red carpet only two minutes before my escort rode up. In the Durbar amphitheatre there were 4,000 special guests, 70,000 spectators on a huge semi-circular mound and 35,000 troops. All of these had a good view of the proceedings. I felt really proud of the general appearance of the Durbar and its surroundings.

As soon as the King and Queen, wearing their crowns and royal robes, had taken their seats on their thrones the Durbar commenced and was led off by myself kneeling and kissing the King's hand. I was followed by the Members of my Council, the Governors and Lieutenant-Governors, who came up in groups and after bowing returned to their places. These were followed by the Ruling Chiefs and Princes, who each made their obeisance in accordance with their own customs, and very varied they were. Certainly the nicest was that of the Rajput Chiefs, who all of them knelt down and presented their swords for the King to touch.

Quite at the beginning an incident occurred which excited much hostile comment and created a great stir. The Gaekwar of Baroda had on his arrival at the Durbar appeared in the usual Mahratta dress covered with priceless jewels. Immediately before the arrival of Their Majesties he was seen to take off all his jewels and when he, the third Maharaja in rank, approached to make his obeisance to the King it was noticed that he was wearing the ordinary white linen everyday dress of a Mahratta with only a walking-stick in his hand. He made a very inadequate obeisance and turning round abruptly walked back to his seat. His lack of good manners contrasted with the conspicuous courtesy of his brother Princes. During the next few days everybody was wondering what notice I intended to take of this incident, and to those who inquired of me I merely said, " You will see later." These words would, I knew, be repeated to the Gaekwar who, from my knowledge of his psychology, I felt sure would be getting more frightened every day at my inaction. Finally, about a week later, he wrote and asked if I would receive him saying there had been a misunderstanding as to his attitude at the Durbar which he would like to explain. I refused to receive him until he had addressed me a full apology in terms satisfactory to myself for his attitude of disrespect to the King at the Durbar for which there could be no possible explanation that he could offer. He pressed me to receive him, but I maintained my refusal and in the end I received a full apology. I would add as an explanation of my firmness towards him that the Gaekwar had the record in that when in Europe he associated with Indian extremists who could not return to India and his State was a hot-bed of sedition and contained printing presses where seditious literature was printed for dissemination throughout India.

It was in the last stage of the Durbar when the King and Queen had returned from the central thrones where I had announced the boons conferred on the people of India in com-memoration of their accession, and had resumed their seats on the thrones where they had received obeisance, that I handed to H.M. a document which had been carefully prepared an-nouncing the transfer of the capital from Calcutta to Delhi, the reunion of Eastern and Western Bengal and other administrative changes. The King rose and read the statement in a clear voice which was heard distinctly by all the 4,000 principal Durbaris present. It came like a bombshell. At the first moment there was a deep silence of profound surprise, followed in a few seconds by a wild burst of cheering. At the same time the Government officials broke the seals of the packets of the Official Gazette prepared beforehand in the " Mystery Camp " and distributed them broadcast throughout the amphi-theatre. For the next few days there was no other subject of discussion in the camp, while the Indian Press was full of it. The Bengalis of the two Bengals were enthusiastic over the reunion of their province, of which the partition had been forced upon them by Lord Curzon, and though they would of course have preferred that Calcutta should remain the Capital so that they might still be able to exercise the same undue in-fluence on the Viceroy's Council and in the Legislative Assembly that they had exercised in the past, they were sharp enough to realize that the advantages of reunion outweighed the disadvan-tage of the change of capital to Delhi, and they regarded the change as an act of great statesmanship and reconciliation on the part of the Sovereign. On the other hand, the British mercantile community in Calcutta and elsewhere in Bengal was simply rabid, and no words were too bad for me, who was naturally regarded as the principal author and offender. Their real reasons were very petty. They resented Calcutta becoming a provincial capital instead of the capital of India, and the removal to Delhi of the Viceregal Court with all its State and ceremony, which would naturally be followed by the transfer of the Commander-in-Chief and his staff and the members of the Viceroy's Council together with the staffs of all the Government Departments. The agitation raised in Calcutta to set aside the King's announcement was violent and with the support of Lansdowne, Curzon and Minto in the House of Lords was kept up during the whole of my stay in India. No effort was spared to put a spoke in my wheel, and though I passed through some difficult times I defeated the opposition. On opening my morning paper, the *Statesman* of Calcutta, shortly after my return there, I noticed the leading article with a heading "H.M.G." Thinking this an expression of the views of the paper on His Majesty's Government, I took no notice of it till I happened to catch sight of my name lower down in the article, when I found to my amusement that H.M.G. meant "Hardinge must go". I met one of the editors a few days later and told him that I quite agreed, but from Calcutta only.

Throughout the rest of India the change was enthusiastically greeted, and particularly by the Ruling Chiefs, who would naturally be in much closer contact with the Viceroy in a central position at Delhi than at Calcutta, which was a cul-de-sac. An interesting point of view was that of many Indians who regarded the change of capital as a definite intimation on the part of England of an intention to remain permanently in India and of her power to maintain herself, since Calcutta had originally become the seat of the Government of India only because of the possibility of removal by sea in the event of an outbreak or revolution.

Although I myself did not see it, being otherwise occupied, I was told that after the King and Queen had left the central thrones there was a rush of Indians to the spot, who kissed the thrones and even the ground where Their Majesties had stood. Such is the veneration in India of the King their Sovereign.

After the Durbar was over, when I had just returned to my tent to change my uniform, I received a message that the King wished to see me. I went at once to H.M.'s tent and was received by him in his State dress but without the robes, and he expressed to me his thanks, his congratulations on the great success of the Durbar and his warm appreciation of the preparations made and of the manner in which everything had been carried out. I must say I was deeply touched and greatly gratified by the warmth of his approval, which was far more than I had ever anticipated or hoped.

The State Investiture was quite one of the most interesting functions that took place in an enormous *shamiana* (marquee) erected in the camp to hold about a thousand people seated. There were altogether about 150 recipients of honours to be invested by the King. H.M. had suggested appearing in the robes of a Knight Grand Cross of the Star of India, but I protested and insisted on his wearing his robes of the Garter, since my position as Grand Master of the Order of the Star of India entailed wearing more magnificent robes than those of a Grand Cross. He finally agreed to do so.

The day before the investiture took place I suggested to H.M. that since the Queen was already a Knight of the Garter it would be very suitable to the occasion that she should also be made a Knight Grand Cross of the Star of India, and he approved but wished it to be kept as a surprise till the actual moment for investiture arrived, but naturally I made in advance all the necessary arrangements. As soon as all the official recipients of the G.C.S.I. had been invested I rose from my place on the King's right and having made a bow to the Queen led her out of the tent to the great surprise of everybody, who could not imagine what was taking place. In the anteroom of the tent the Queen put on the robes of a Knight Grand Cross

THE INVESTITURE, IMPERIAL DURBAR
From a painting by G. P. Jacomb Hood, M.V.O.

and I then led H.M. back into the tent straight up to the King, who invested her with the insignia of the Order. The Queen's re-entry into the tent wearing the robes of the Order was very loudly cheered.

One other incident occurred of a somewhat alarming nature. When the ceremony was only half-finished a cry arose of fire, and one of my A.D.C.s told me at once that one of the tents near by had caught fire and that it was being rapidly pulled down. The alarm spread to the audience, who began to leave their places, but I stopped this at once by shouting out, " Sit down ! Nobody is to leave his place." The King and Queen behaved admirably and did not move an inch, and panic was almost immediately averted by the news that all danger was over. An inquiry was made as to how the fire had arisen and it appeared that some messenger bringing a letter had propped his bicycle with a lighted lamp against the tent and had left it there. The result was that the tent of Lord Crewe's private secretary, with its contents, was entirely destroyed.

During their stay in the camp the King and Queen expressed to me their wish to lay the foundation-stones of the new capital of India. The proposal presented considerable difficulty since it was then an open question as to where the site of the new city would really be found. Still, I was of opinion that it was very desirable that such a ceremony should be associated with the King and Queen even if it proved necessary to move later the stones elsewhere to where the new city would be built, as was eventually done. Consequently I arranged the function and the foundation-stones were laid with great ceremony within the precincts of the camp and before a large crowd by the King and Queen. It proved later that the site on which they were laid was not that selected for the new capital and a year afterwards I had these stones quietly removed and placed in an honoured position in the secretariat building in the new city.

The Calcutta opponents of the scheme once more showed

their bad taste by promulgating a story that the foundation-stones laid by the King and Queen were tombstones and thereby tried to inspire the Indian mind, always sensitive to such insinuations, with the idea that the new city was foredoomed to be unlucky. I need hardly say that there was not one word of truth in this calumny, and that the foundation-stones had been actually selected by the Member of Council for Public Works and had been cut from a large block. Lord Ronaldshay[1] repeated this allegation in a speech in the House of Commons, so I wrote to him expressing to him my surprise at his making such a statement and insisted on his public withdrawal of it. This he did.

One of the most spectacular events during the period of the Durbar was the review of 50,000 troops by the King. The line of troops stretched for nearly four miles. The most picturesque and striking incident was the march past of four Highland regiments in solid brigade formation. Their splendid appearance excited the wildest enthusiasm. The young Maharaja of Jodhpur, one of the King's pages, mounted on a white Arab pony at the head of the Jodhpur Lancers, and the Nawab of Bahawalpur, aged 7, on a camel at the head of his Camel Corps, created a great sensation. The only amusing incident was that when the Commander-in-Chief, having passed the King, turned and cantered to stand behind His Majesty, his horse, that he had borrowed from the Maharaja Scindia, bucked and nearly threw him, his medals and decorations being scattered over the ground !

There was yet one more function amongst the many that seems worth mentioning. There was a large and numerously attended garden party in the gardens of the Fort which, as stated earlier, had been transformed from a dusty waste into a lovely garden. It had been previously mentioned by Sir Louis Dane, Lieutenant-Governor of the Punjab, that the people of the Province would wish to pay their respects to the King and Queen,

[1] Afterwards 2nd Marquess of Zetland.

so it was arranged that Their Majesties should, during an interval
of the garden party, don their crowns and royal robes and sit
in a conspicuous position on the battlements of the fort from
which the people in the *bela* or park below would be able to see
them. It was a very successful suggestion. The people came
in from the villages in thousands, were marshalled in the park
below the fort and passed before the King and Queen in huge
masses and in perfect order, cheering Their Majesties as they
passed. It was calculated that more than 100,000 people passed
during the $1\frac{1}{2}$ hours devoted to the procession. Nothing could
have been better in every way.

On the 16th December the King and Queen left Delhi; the
King going to Nepal to shoot tigers with the Maharaja, in which
he was eminently successful, while the Queen went for a tour
in Rajputana, where it had been arranged that she should visit
several Ruling Chiefs. Her tour proved a complete success and
she enjoyed it greatly.

It had been my intention to go to Dehra Dun with several
of my guests during the necessary interval before the King and
Queen came to stay with me in Government House, Calcutta,
but in view of a case of cholera having occurred in an adjoining
village I decided to go instead to Barrackpore. This had the
great advantage of enabling me personally to supervise from
close at hand the necessary preparations to receive the King and
Queen at Government House, Calcutta, with an enormous staff
of officials and servants in addition to my own guests and staff.
It was a stupendous task, as may be understood when I state that
during those ten days in Calcutta we were seventy people to
breakfast, lunch and dinner every day (not counting other
guests by special invitation) and 150 English servants, clerks and
maids who were housed in tents in the grounds and had two
separate mess tents. The amount of food and drink consumed
during the stay of Their Majesties with me was simply
stupendous, but it was the 150 servants whom it was difficult
for my Controller to satisfy. It was a period of great strain

for my establishment, who acquitted themselves in a really marvellous manner.

The King and Queen arrived by train at Calcutta on the 30th December and I met them at the Howrah railway station and accompanied them on board the Port Commissioner's steamer *Howrah*, which proceeded to Prince's Ghat, some two miles down the river, where Their Majesties landed. This course was adopted to avoid passing through a number of narrow streets to Government House, where inadequate opportunities for the population to take part in the official arrival of Their Majesties in Calcutta would have been presented. The acting Lieutenant-Governor of Bengal and all the officials of the Presidency were assembled at Prince's Ghat to receive Their Majesties, where an amphitheatre capable of holding 3,000 persons had been erected, together with a canopy and dais where Their Majesties received an address from the Corporation of Calcutta. After replying to the address Their Majesties proceeded in State carriages to Government House, a distance of about two miles, vast crowds along the route giving them an enthusiastic welcome. In the meantime Winifred and I had returned by a shorter route in order to receive Their Majesties at Government House, where all the officials of the Government of India had already assembled and were in due course presented.

The following day being Sunday, Their Majesties attended divine service at the Cathedral and on the 2nd January the usual Proclamation Parade was held on the *maidan* by the King.

I do not propose to describe the many fêtes that took place in Calcutta in celebration of Their Majesties' visit, such as the race-meeting, garden party, horse show, investiture, etc., except to mention the very successful torchlight tattoo organized by Major Brancker, R.A., and the Native Pageant. The torch-light tattoo was far better than the one in Delhi, thanks to the skill and initiative of the organizer, afterwards Sir Sefton Brancker of the Imperial Air Force. That evening the whole of Calcutta

THE KING AND QUEEN ARRIVING IN CALCUTTA WITH LORD AND
LADY HARDINGE IN THE BACKGROUND

was brilliantly illuminated and great pressure was put upon me to persuade the King and Queen to drive through the streets and to receive a purely Indian welcome, but I flatly declined as I considered the risk too great. As for the pageant, it was one of the most successful and interesting displays during Their Majesties' tour in India. It was purely Indian in character, with Indian music, dances, mock battles, processions with elephants, etc. It was witnessed by nearly a million people. After the departure of Their Majesties the crowd burst the barriers, and the curious sight was again witnessed of Indians kissing the ground where Their Majesties had stood, and carrying off with them small handfuls of dust from the proximity of the thrones. These were ten of the most strenuous days of my life, as I had to supervise and provide for every moment of the day for my royal guests, but everything passed off without a hitch and to Their Majesties' complete satisfaction.

On the evening before the departure of Their Majesties the King bestowed upon me the Royal Victoria Chain, a very high and rare honour. At dinner that evening Their Majesties with their staff and I with mine being the only persons present, there were three large and very beautiful silver centrepieces on the table, of which for some time I took no notice, thinking that they formed part of the official plate of the Viceroy. During a pause I noticed with surprise that the silver piece nearest me bore my own coat of arms, and drawing it to me, I read an inscription upon it showing that these three splendid pieces were a present to myself from the King. The fact that I had not noticed these centrepieces was a source of much amusement and chaff.

It was during that last evening of their stay at Government House that the King told me that it was his hope and desire that he would be able to send his sons successively to India to occupy the post of Viceroy, and he invited my opinion upon it. I replied that, in the first place, the post of Viceroy was extremely arduous and needed a person accustomed to deal with official work both political and administrative, and that the education of a royal prince seemed to me hardly a sufficient preparation. To this the King at once said that a Prince, as Viceroy, could have some high official with a recognized position who would carry on the official and administrative work for the Viceroy. To this argument I answered that the Viceroy, as Head of the Government of India and the Representative of the Sovereign was, and always had been subject to criticism and attack from various·sources, and I could conceive nothing more likely to diminish the existing prestige of the Royal Family in India than to expose a Royal Prince to such criticism, while if the official work of the Viceroy was performed by a sort of Prime Minister it would end by the latter being regarded as the fount of honour and the real Viceroy. I stated my opinion quite clearly that such an idea was quite impracticable unless a Prince could be found really capable of tackling and dealing satisfactorily with the . overwhelming work of the Viceroy, a condition never likely to be realized.

The royal party left by train on January 8th with the same procedure as on their arrival and embarked for Bombay on their special train. I left in another train immediately afterwards, and, by previous arrangement, passed the royal train on the road so as to be in time to receive Their Majesties on their arrival at Bombay. My train arrived at its destination half an hour before the royal train and Their Majesties drove straight to the harbour in procession, where they were received by Sir George Clarke, the Governor, and his Legislative Council, who presented an address to the King.

The King and Queen having bid farewell to those present and acknowledged the salutations of the large number of troops and spectators drawn up in serried ranks to witness their departure, embarked in the royal barge of H.M.S. *Medina*. My own launch was lying alongside to take me on board, but the King insisted on my coming with him in his barge. Their Majesties were visibly affected at leaving India, where they had spent a really happy time, and I am afraid my own face betrayed the

THE KING AND QUEEN DRIVING ALONG THE RED ROAD TO CALCUTTA

satisfaction I felt at the close of all my responsibility for their safety from the moment they set foot on the royal barge, which was technically British soil, for the King suddenly said to me : " You seem very pleased, Charlie, to be getting rid of us ! " " Not at all, sir," I replied, " I should be more than pleased if your Majesties would stay in India for another six weeks, but I am of course very happy to feel that your visit has been, such a complete success and without the smallest incident of an un-toward character of any kind." The King replied, " Yes, I can well understand your responsibility and anxieties during the past six weeks, which must have been heavy all the time."

I lunched on board the *Medina* with Their Majesties, and when the hour for sailing approached I asked permission to take leave of Their Majesties. The King expressed the wish that I should remain for a quarter of an hour after all the other guests had left. I did not until later understand why. I re-mained talking with Their Majesties in their cabin until an officer came to announce that my launch was alongside. Their Majesties accompanied me on to the deck, where I took leave of them, and I found a guard of honour of Royal Marines drawn up with their band, who saluted and played while I descended the companion ladder, and as my launch bearing the Viceroy's flag passed the escorting British cruisers they fired a salute in my honour. I feel quite sure that the King had heard of the dis-courteous manner in which I had been received on his arrival six weeks earlier and had determined that on his departure it should be otherwise.

A few days afterwards I received the following telegram from the King at Aden : " Before leaving Indian waters the Queen and I desire again to acknowledge with sincere gratitude all you have done for us during our most happy and never-to-be-forgotten stay in India, and at the same time to congratulate you heartily upon the admirable manner in which everything in connection with our visit was planned and carried out." To receive such a charming telegram was indeed a crowning source of pleasure.

CHAPTER V

CALCUTTA: DELHI: OFFICIAL VISITS, 1912

DURING the two days that I spent resting at Bombay after the King's departure I had an interview with Lovat Fraser, who appeared to be much upset over the reversal at the Durbar of the partition of Bengal. After some conversation I gathered that what annoyed him was that he had just published a book on Curzon's administration in India, in which he had proclaimed the partition of Bengal to have been Curzon's greatest administrative success. I sympathized with him that his book should have been published just at the very moment when this so-called success was reversed ! Of course I knew nothing at the time of this publication, but it must have had the effect of embittering Curzon still more.

The following three months, the last that I was to spend in Calcutta as my official residence, were very fully occupied with the development of the scheme for the transfer of the capital to Delhi and the creation of a new Presidency Government in Bengal which entailed the delimitation of new provincial boundaries, the appointment of a Governor for Bengal, a Lieutenant-Governor for Behar and Orissa, and a Commissioner for Assam, with their respective executive councils and many other complicated administrative questions. In the meantime I experienced a loss that I felt very deeply. During my absence in Bombay, Sir John Jenkins, the Home Member of my Council, died from cerebral hæmorrhage during an attack of fever, and I was only in time on my return to Calcutta to attend his funeral. He was a man for whose loyalty and ability I had the greatest admiration, and although on my first arrival in India we had a few differences of opinion, this was entirely changed when he

Farewell to India : Lord Hardinge goes Ashore,
having taken leave of the King and Queen on board H.M.S. "Medina"
immediately before Their Majesties' departure for home

realized how anxious I was to work with him for the good of the country, and ever afterwards I only met with the most loyal support. His death at that time created a situation of some difficulty, since he had the whole question of the provincial boundaries and the new distribution of personnel at his finger-ends. As time pressed I sent at once for Sir Reginald Craddock, Chief Commissioner of the Central Provinces, to fill his place, and appointed Sir Benjamin Robertson as his successor at Nagpur. Although Craddock was an able administrator and a loyal colleague, he was very " sunbaked " and reactionary in his ideas. Robertson's appointment proved excellent in every way.

As regards the new Governorship of Bengal, I had been anxious that it should be given to Lord Southborough, but he declined the offer on grounds of delicate health, of which I was unaware. It was eventually decided to transfer Lord Carmichael to Calcutta from Madras, where he had only just taken up his appointment as Governor, and Lord Pentland was appointed by the Home Government to Madras.

When the decision had first been taken to move the capital from Calcutta to Delhi it had been the wish of the King that the Viceroy should retain Government House at Calcutta as his residence and that he should visit Calcutta every cold weather for a few weeks. It was proposed that the Governor should live at Belvedere, the former residence of the Lieutenant-Governor. After I had been a few weeks in Calcutta I realized that to leave Government House vacant for nearly the whole year, and for the Governor to occupy a very inadequate residence, was a policy that could not be defended, especially as the Viceroy could still retain Barrackpore as his residence when he wished to visit Calcutta. Consequently I obtained the King's permission to surrender Government House to the newly appointed Governor and to retain Barrackpore, which I agreed to lend to the Governor for his use as a week-end resort. It was also Carmichael's wish that I should not come too often at first to Calcutta since the Governor would necessarily be overshadowed by the Viceroy. I thus cut the painter completely from Calcutta, and during my four succeeding years in India I only went three times to Calcutta, paying one official visit to the Governor as his guest and on the other two occasions staying a few days at Barrackpore, where I entertained Calcutta society, to their complete satisfaction, and from where I performed my official duties in Calcutta such as those pertaining to the Chancellor of the University, etc. I have a very happy memory of Barrackpore with its wonderful banyan tree with varied orchids growing from its branches covering more than an acre of ground and under which I gave many dinners of over fifty people. My successors gave up Barrackpore and took Belvedere as their residence, going there every Christmas for a month. I know the Governors dislike the arrangement, while it seems hardly right that the Viceroy should be less well housed than the Governor, and the move from Delhi to Calcutta and back naturally costs a large sum of money. It is at Christmas that Calcutta has its principal gathering of the year with races, polo tournament, etc., and it is hard luck on the Governor that at this particular moment of the year the Viceroy should descend in state on Calcutta and completely overshadow the Governor. I know how bitter the Governors since my time feel about it.

Of the large collection of furniture and of pictures of former Viceroys and Governors-General I took away from Calcutta only those pictures that were of former Governors-General and Viceroys, leaving all those of former Governors of Bengal and such other pictures as had no Viceregal connection. Lord Curzon tried to raise objections to the Viceregal pictures being moved from Calcutta in the hope that they might be relegated to the Victoria Memorial, but as they were absolutely the official property of the Viceroy I refused to listen to his objections and acted accordingly. Any pictures that the Government of Bengal wished to retain were copied for them in England and sent out to Calcutta, so that the new Governor walked into a completely furnished house.

64

Owing to the chaos that prevailed in the Military Department I succeeded in arranging with the Home Government that a Commission under the Presidency of Field-Marshal Lord Nicholson should sit in India upon the question of the military organization and expenditure of the Army in India. A Royal Commission was also sent out from home under the Chairmanship of Lord Islington to sit upon the organization of the Civil Service in India. Both these Commissioners met in India during the course of 1912. Neither of them was productive of satisfactory results, though much light was thrown upon the subjects under discussion.

Towards the end of January I visited Eastern Bengal and its capital Dacca. I met with a more enthusiastic reception there than anywhere, which was a remarkable testimony of the satisfaction of the people at the reunion of the Province of Bengal. I received numerous deputations and gave great satisfaction by the promise of a new university at Dacca and of certain educational advantages justified by the progress of the Province. I stayed with the Lieutenant-Governor, Sir Charles Bayley, whom I had selected as the Lieutenant-Governor of the newly created Province of Behar and Orissa. One of the most unpleasant reminiscences that I have of Dacca is the size and number of its mosquitoes. They made life a burden, and I was reduced to doing my work sitting on my bed under a mosquito-net. At night their singing was almost like a band !

A few weeks later I visited Benares and Lucknow. Benares was very interesting from a Hindu religious point of view and the Ghats very picturesque, but nothing could be more insanitary since the drains of the town flow into the river while the people bathe and drink the water. As Viceroy I was given the privilege of entering the most sacred Hindu temple of Benares. I also visited the Hindu temple at Gaya and took cuttings of the tree under which Buddha is reported to have sat. I sent these home but heard no more of them.

Lucknow was the best town I had so far seen in India. It was very refreshing to find what a much wider outlook people in the northern provinces had than the people of Calcutta, who mostly knowing nothing of India could only regard Indian affairs from a purely Calcutta point of view. I am not exaggerating when I state that a large percentage of the English and foreign population of Calcutta knew only Bombay, where they landed, and Calcutta where they lived. That was sufficient for them. We enjoyed greatly our stay in Lucknow and were deeply interested in all the historic reminiscences of the defence of the Residency during the Indian Mutiny.

In the meantime the question of the reunion of Bengal and the transfer of the capital was raised in the House of Lords by Curzon, who attacked the scheme with a bitterness that was so unrelieved as really to damage its effectiveness. No ordinary person could well believe that the Government of India with the approval of the Home Government would be such a pack of fools as " to produce a large and complex scheme without a single touch of merit or wisdom " (these were his words), especially in view of the chorus of approval in India except from the English of Calcutta. He was supported by Minto, who used the well-worn criticism of " concessions to agitation ", and by Lansdowne, who was only mildly critical and urged the House to accept the fact and to " make it a success ". All the ex-Governors, Reay, Ampthill, Harris and McDonnell, were favourable and Lord Morley made an excellent speech in favour of the scheme. Curzon made a deplorable mistake in retailing a story to the effect that the Nawab of Dacca, in disgust at the reunion of Bengal, had refused a decoration that had been bestowed upon him by the King, a story without the slightest foundation, which was easily refuted by Crewe. This spoilt still further the effect of his speech. Curzon did not accept Lansdowne's advice to make the scheme a success, for during the whole of the rest of my time in India he never missed an opportunity to endeavour to obstruct and destroy the scheme, but he failed as it was too palpable to everybody that his opposition was based entirely on personal grounds.

It was at this time that Crewe appointed a small Committee consisting of Captain Swinton, former member of the London County Council, Lutyens, the distinguished architect, and Brodie, a sanitary engineer of Liverpool, to come out to India to study the question of the site for the new capital at Delhi and to decide where it should be. I welcomed the idea and they arrived at Delhi in the spring and spent some weeks wandering round the outskirts of Delhi on an elephant and failed, as will eventually be shown, to find an acceptable site. It must have been very hot work !

At this time general peace prevailed in Bengal such as had not existed for seven or eight years previously, murders and anarchy having ceased while the whole of India was prosperous and busy harvesting a record crop. There is no doubt that the King's visit to India and his pronouncements at the Durbar had had a most pacifying effect.

On the 27th March, 1912, I made my official departure from Calcutta. Immense and most enthusiastic crowds of Indians lined the streets the whole way to Howrah station and gave me a veritable ovation. This demonstration was a mark of gratitude on the part of the Bengalis for the reunion of Bengal, which to them was of far greater importance than the transfer of the capital to Delhi. Although the British residents came in numbers to Government House to bid me farewell, they did not fail to continue to show their chagrin over the change of capital, which some of them in conversation frankly admitted entailed no material loss upon them, except loss of prestige in Calcutta becoming a provincial capital, and the absence of the Viceregal Court, with all the paraphernalia of levees, courts, A.D.C.s. etc. Although I fully realized that my future accommodation at Delhi would necessarily be inadequate and uncomfortable, and although I liked Calcutta and its surroundings, I was, on the whole, not sorry to leave until the English residents had become accustomed to the changes.

A thunderstorm broke as we left Government House, and as

some correspondent with a nautical turn of mind reported that as I left " the Viceroy's flag was struck ", the English Press of Calcutta endeavoured to spread amongst the superstitious the fable that my flag had been struck by lightning as a mark of the displeasure of Providence at the change of capital ! It is curious how hard it is to kill such lies, for I heard this and the story of the foundation-stones of Delhi being tombstones repeated when I visited India twenty years later.

As for the two principal English journals of Calcutta, the *Statesman* and the *Englishman*, from the time of the Durbar and until after my departure from Calcutta, the virulence of their attacks upon me and my administration were without precedent, one of them likening me to the infamous " Suraj-ud-Dowleh ", known as " the scourge of Bengal ". So much so that Crewe in a speech in the House of Lords referred to their seditious attitude, which evoked a protest from these Calcutta journals. To this Crewe very properly replied that the press laws in force in India applied to the English Press equally with the Indian Press. My policy, which repaid me over and over again, was to treat these attacks with complete indifference, a course which enraged the Calcutta Press and amused me, one of these journals ingenuously remarking in an article that nothing that they said appeared to disturb the Viceroy " who went his own way ".

Just before I left Calcutta an awkward and unpleasant incident occurred. My carriage was at the door and I was saying good-bye to my friends when the Lieutenant-Governor of Bengal brought me the Orissa Tenancy and Mining Law passed by the Bengal Legislative Council on the previous day and asked my assent to it. Now in four days' time Orissa was to be separated from Bengal and embodied in the new province of Behar and Orissa, and it was fairly evident that the Bill had been rushed through the Council with a view to getting it passed before the change of provincial boundaries in order to meet the interests of Bengali landowners which I knew to be considerable. As it was contrary to my practice to give my assent to a measure which I had not had an opportunity to consider maturely, and in view of the objections mentioned above, I refused my assent after consultation with my legal advisers. The Bengali landowners were greatly annoyed when my refusal became known, while on the other hand the inhabitants of Orissa were truly grateful. There had been no instance of a Viceroy withholding his assent to a Bill for a great number of years. Later on I was thanked by the Orissa Council for my action, while Lord Carmichael, the newly appointed Governor of Bengal, approved it, and even Sir W. Duke, who had pressed me to give my assent, came round to the opinion that my refusal was " not unnatural ".

From Calcutta I went to Patiala for a state visit of three days which was most enjoyable, and I then continued my journey to Peshawar, where I stayed for a few days with Roos-Keppel, the Chief Commissioner, a remarkable frontier officer. From Peshawar I visited the Khyber, Landi Kotal, Malakand, the valley of the Swat River, Kohat and Samana. When at Landi Kotal, where one is surrounded by mountains and can see nothing beyond the Afghan frontier post, I expressed a wish to have a view from some high hill over the plain of Jellalabad in the direction of Cabul. This was arranged by handing me over to the protection and care of the Shinwari tribe, who mustered in thousands and running fully armed by the side of my horse, accompanied me to the top of a hill from which I had a splendid view and could see Dacca and Jellalabad with the Cabul River winding along the plain, and in the far distance the Hindu Kush rising up beyond. It was an unforgettable sight. To ensure my safety, every hillside for miles was occupied by Shinwaris, and with true hospitality they roasted a sheep for my luncheon on the hillside and gave me some quaint arms as souvenirs. The Shinwaris were a very wild and picturesque lot of tribesmen, armed to the teeth, wild as hawks but with a natural grace and self-confidence. They impressed me favourably. They returned me safely to the British post at Landi

Kotal. (They have since been in revolt against the Ameer and have attacked Jellalabad.)

It was at Landi Kotal that I came first into personal contact with Mr. Maffey, the Political Officer who impressed me most favourably as a very able official with an exceptional aptitude for dealing with Mahomedans, and I did all I could during my stay in India to push him forward. He was afterwards Sir John Maffey, Governor-General of the Sudan, and there could not have been a better or more suitable appointment.[1]

It was at Malakand that I saw what is done only by British administrators in India. A marvellous tunnel two miles in length through a mountain to carry canal water for the benefit chiefly of tribes outside our border had just been completed. We were also holding small forts for miles beyond our frontier for the purpose of keeping the roads open and maintaining the *pax Britannica* upon our borders. There the tribesmen may shoot each other as much as they like, provided there is no interference with the roads. This is so fully recognized by the warring tribesmen that all roads and fifty yards on each side are recognized by them as neutral territory.

I visited Fort Lockhart at Samana and learnt there that the tribesmen had been troublesome with snipers from neighbouring towers, but that the Indian battalion quartered in the fort had, in view of my impending visit, succeeded in extirpating all the snipers with rifle fire.

On my way back from the North-West Frontier I opened the Upper Chenab Canal, which had been seven years under construction and had cost two millions sterling. It was part of a triple project to cost eight millions, and estimated to bring in a return of 8 per cent. It was a wonderful sight to see the immense wave of water rush down the canal, bearing in its wake a flood of agricultural abundance and prosperity to desert lands, after I had simply touched an electric button opening the sluices. The Maharaja of Kashmir and all the high

[1] He was created Lord Rugby in 1947.

officials of the Government of the Punjab were present at the ceremony.

From there I went to Dehra Dun and into camp on the banks of the Ganges for rest and shooting. During my ten days in camp with my Private Secretary and two A.D.C.s, we shot three tigers, one leopard and 21 stags, mostly with good heads. One evening in camp the wind was blowing from a spot where a tiger was being skinned and the smell was very unpleasant. I sent word that the carcase of the tiger must be removed within the hour. Before that period had elapsed hundreds of villagers could be seen going off with bits of tiger in baskets and even in official envelopes till none was left. Next morning the headman of the village came to see me, quite a nice young man, and I asked him what the villagers did with tiger's meat. He told me that tiger's fat was the best remedy for rheumatism, that dried tiger flesh was a certain cure for consumption or pneumonia in children, but the part of the tiger most prized was the whiskers, which the villagers cut up very small and gave in small doses to their children to make them brave ! This explained why my Indian servants continually pulled out the whiskers of my tiger skins until they were told that the hairs had been counted ! From Dehra Dun I went straight to Simla. Winifred was with me in camp and enjoyed greatly fishing for mahseer in the Ganges, and with some success.

The following five months at Simla were spent in real hard work in a cool atmosphere without the disturbance of Calcutta dissensions. I had a great deal of work in connection with new Delhi and paid several visits to that city to supervise the building of temporary quarters for the Government offices, to discuss the question of the site of the new city, the appointment of architects, and the style of architecture to be incorporated in the new city. At the same time I took steps to create the new Delhi enclave to be administered directly by the Government of India and independently of any local or provincial government. Further, I supervised plans for the improvement of the old city of Delhi by remedying the defective sanitation of the city, clearing the pest of flies, laying out gardens and lawns, mending the roads and beautifying the surroundings of all the most famous monuments. Two important decisions were taken; first, that the site should be on the southern side of Delhi, and second, that it should be at Raisina. It was I myself who decided the latter point after several visits to various possible sites. The incident is worth recording.

Having been informed that Crewe's committee of experts had selected and approved a site and that the lay-out had been flagged for my inspection and criticism, I went from Simla to Delhi with a considerable staff of technical experts, including three of the best engineers. The moment I saw the selected site I realized its objections. It would be hot; it had no views; and it had no room for expansion. After consultation for more than two hours I told the assembled staff that I would rather not build a new capital at all than build it on that site. I asked to be left alone for a quarter of an hour before coming to a decision, and at its close I rejected the site as impossible. I then mounted and asked Hailey (later Sir Malcolm and then Lord Hailey, Governor of the United Provinces), Commissioner of Delhi, to accompany me to choose a new site, and we galloped over the plain to a hill some distance away. From the top of the hill there was a magnificent view embracing old Delhi and all the principal monuments situated outside the town, with the River Jumma winding its way like a silver streak in the foreground at a little distance. I said at once to Hailey, "This is the site for Government House", and he readily agreed. On examination I observed that the area of the top of the hill was hardly adequate for a fine Government House with all its necessary adjuncts, but one of the engineers who was present said at once that there would be no difficulty in cutting off the top of the hill so as to make a fine and broad base for building upon. The idea struck me as novel, but it was confirmed and accepted by all and the site adopted. It was equally approved by the experts from England.

72

There were many other questions that occupied my attention during my stay at Simla, such as the Nicholson Commission upon military organization in India, a mission to report upon indentured emigration in the Colonies which I entrusted to Mr. McNeil, an official of the Indian Civil Service who was later Governor of the Irish Free State, and problems connected with the Nizam's Administration and some of the other native states. For the solution of these I always invited the Ruling Chiefs to come and stay with me at Simla to'discuss them, a proceeding which we all mutually enjoyed.

In the middle of October I paid an official visit to Kashmir, which was most enjoyable. The arrival in a State barge, the river-bank being packed with crowds in brilliant clothing was a wonderful spectacle. It was my grandfather who had placed the grandfather of the actual Maharaja upon the throne of Kashmir and for that reason he always called me his " cousin " and never ceased to tell me of his gratitude to my family. According to precedent he had to offer me a very heavy tribute of several thousands of rupees which were placed in bags on the lawn of the Residency and guarded by troops. As a joke I told my Military Secretary to remove them and the old man seemed quite relieved when I merely touched a bag and remitted to him the whole sum. He used to be incoherent at certain times of the day until he had taken his opium pill, and he then, became quite amusing. At the conclusion of my ceremonial visit I went off by myself with my servants to a hut that the Maharaja had built specially for me on the edge of a trout stream in the middle of a forest. I had the most wonderful sport stalking and killed six large stags in four days. The Maharaja disapproved of stalking and had 1,000 beaters in camp at some distance to drive for me, but I had no use for them. In addition I had two days' duck shooting with my party, in which we killed 1,890 duck and geese, and one day's partridge driving on the slopes of a mountain in which we killed 130 brace of partridges.

On one occasion when travelling with the Maharaja he insisted upon my visiting a group of fine sycamore trees by the road-side and on my sitting upon a seat placed beneath the biggest tree. I could not understand his insistence until just before leaving I walked to the other side of the tree and saw carved upon the trunk a long inscription of how I had rested under the tree and enjoyed the hospitality of its shade ! I laughed when I thought of his insistence.

From Kashmir I paid official visits to Indore and Udaipur the most beautiful city, capital of the most backward state in India. On my arrival I learnt that the Maharana was ill but most anxious that I should invest him with the G.C.I.E. that had been conferred upon him. He is regarded as the most fanatical and orthodox Hindu and is supposed to be descended from the sun. After my arrival the Resident told me that one of his gardeners had been sentenced on the previous day to 10 years' imprisonment for striking with the scabbard of his sword a sacred bull that was devouring the supplies on the counter of a greengrocer's shop. The bull suffered no hurt. I sent word to the Maharana that I considered such a sentence excessive and that he had better revise it before I came to see him. The sentence was reduced to one year's imprisonment, which was even excessive, but one had to take into account the religious fanaticism of the ruler.

The investiture was more than unusual. I was conducted to the roof of his palace by a very narrow stone staircase by which only one person could mount at a time and which was guarded by two men armed with axes at the top. I found the Maharana sitting on the edge of his low bed under a large awning on what was practically the roof of the palace, in a very dishevelled state with bare feet, a white bandage round his head and a fur dressing-gown. The only other article of furniture was a chair for myself. His ministers were present and everything I said to the Maharana was conveyed to him through these Ministers one after the other, the last holding his hands before the Maharana's ear so that his breath should not reach the Maharana. The room was, however, full of people, whose bare feet I could see below the screens placed round the walls. He was very pleased to receive his Order, but the ribbon and star of the G.C.I.E. looked strange on his shabby dressing-gown. During the visit all the palaces in the lake were illuminated, making a wonderful and fairylike picture, and we were present at an interesting but cruel show of contests between different wild animals. A little of this went a long way, but I was interested to see a wild boar defeat a leopard, without either being seriously hurt.

From Udaipur we went to Jaipur on a State visit, but we stayed with the Resident. Jaipur is a pink city. All the houses and walls are pink, and the effect is very unusual but very good. It has a fine appearance but there is a good deal of camouflage about the buildings, many of them being merely shells. The Maharaja, a dear old man, had no heir because he had been told once by a soothsayer that if he had an heir he would die, but he had quite a number of illegitimate sons who were very much in the foreground. Plague had been raging in Jaipur for three years, largely owing to the refusal on religious grounds of the Maharaja, a bigoted Hindu, to permit the destruction of rats in the capital. There was a large plague camp some miles outside the city, and, as I had heard that the Maharaja took no interest in the welfare of its inmates, I paid a surprise visit with my personal doctor and inspected the whole camp. It was sad to see those patient Indians dying like flies, and who seemed to be pleased to see that I took an interest in them, even those who evidently were dying. On my return I insisted on the Maharaja making many improvements and on spending more money on the camp, and I saw that it was done. He was rather annoyed at my expedition to the plague camp, but he was always most friendly. I also visited the beautiful old fort of Amber.

I did some pigsticking in Jaipur and nearly had an accident owing to the Maharaja insisting on my riding one of his horses instead of my own. The horse had not sufficient speed, so that I never had complete command over the pig, with the result that as I speared the pig it "jinked" and brought down me and my horse. I was ready for trouble on the ground with the pig, but luckily for me he was dead.

During my visit to Jaipur I decided to pay an official visit of one day to the Nawab of Tonk, a Mahomedan Chief whose small state was about 80 miles distant. He was a gay and amusing old boy and had been to see me at Simla. On that occasion, when sitting next my wife at a big luncheon party, during a lull in the conversation he was heard to say : "How many sons has your Excellency ?" to which she replied, "I have two," He then remarked in a loud voice, "I have fifty-two", and exploded with laughter, in which everybody joined. The Maharaja of Jaipur, being a fanatical Hindu, did not much like my visit to the Mahomedan State of Tonk and provided two very inferior motor-cars for the journey, the car containing my staff being only just able to crawl in. I remarked to the Nawab on arriving that I was dissatisfied with my car, and he at once replied that he would send me back in his own. When a few hours later the time came to leave I found a magnificent and brand-new Rolls-Royce car awaiting me, with an Indian chauffeur in a new uniform covered with gold lace. He drove the car at 50 miles an hour and made the streets of Jaipur hideous with the noise of his horn, so that all the Jaipuris should see him and his car. My conviction is that the Nawab guessed the Maharaja would send me over in a bad car and had arranged to provide a new one for me simply to score off him !

In the meantime I held a Durbar in Tonk and the Nawab offered me three of the most wonderful jewelled swords, which I refused to accept on account of their great value. He was much annoyed and could not understand it, and to console him I accepted a small jewelled box. At the Durbar I saw about twelve of his fifty-two sons and very stalwart they were. After the Durbar he took me to a room where he had a collection of swords of historic interest that, as a connoisseur, he had collected during years, and he asked me to choose for myself any sword that I liked. As I knew how he loved his swords I selected the most ordinary I could find, but he snatched it from my hand and himself chose me a sword which, with a very ordinary scabbard, had a marvellous blade more than 100 years old, the maker having made only twelve in his lifetime. I heard from the Resident that when a similar offer was made to Lord Kitchener he chose the very best sword which had been in the Nawab's family for several generations, and the Nawab never forgave him for this.

From Jaipur we went to Bikaner and it had been arranged that my train should stop in the early morning at a small station near to which the Maharaja was particularly anxious that I should shoot an exceptionally large buck that had been marked down. When my train stopped in the morning the Maharaja was on the platform with all his Sirdars, but I was quite unable to leave my bed as I had high fever from food poisoning in Jaipur. Having heard that I had visited the plague camp in Jaipur, they all disappeared, thinking that I had got the plague ! My train remained in the siding and, in spite of my doctor saying that it would be out of the question, I sent word to the Maharaja that I would have a go at the buck next day. Next morning the fever had left me, and although I was feeling very feeble I went into the desert in the afternoon and after a long stalk shot the buck. I had some wonderful sandgrouse shooting, good buck shooting and some pigsticking. As regards pigsticking, it was the last I had of that exhilarating sport, since the King forbade me to do any more as being too dangerous. The Maharaja was a delightful host.

On leaving Bikaner we went to Bhopal on a State visit when it was a great pleasure to us to be the guests of that most loyal and able ruler the Begum, for whom one could only feel the highest respect. She was a great personality and we became great friends. From there we went back to Delhi for the manœuvres, where I spent three days in the saddle with the troops, which was quite restful after my strenuous efforts during my tour. From Delhi I went to the Central Provinces and lastly to Bhurtpore, the last State visit in the programme before my State entry into the new capital which had been fixed for December 23rd. I had a marvellous day's duck shooting at Bhurtpore. There were 50 guns and we killed 3,511 duck, the birds flying high and being kept always on the move by lines of elephants moving up and down the shallow lake. Instead of dogs I had four naked Imperial Service soldiers to retrieve from the water the duck I shot. I noticed during the first two hours of the shoot that not half the duck I shot were picked up, so I offered an anna (about a penny) for every duck collected, and consequently all my birds were picked up and, I believe, some that had been shot by my neighbours. I shot from what was called " The Viceroy's Bund ", an embankment stretching into the middle of the lake, and the birds came both ways and flew well. I remember that there were no less than thirteen kinds of duck in the bag. On the following morning we arrived at Delhi station.

The Viceroy on Holiday : Sport at Gwalior

CHAPTER VI

DELHI OUTRAGE: OFFICIAL DUTIES AND VISITS, 1913−1914

HERE, in view of what followed, I must write something on the state of India during the year that was closing. Ever since the King's arrival in India, more than a year before, absolute peace had prevailed, not a single political murder having occurred in the interval, while during the three or four years immediately preceding the Durbar the average had been one political murder every fortnight. This was really the best answer to the critics of the King's announcements at the Durbar which had produced immediately a state of peace and content- ment unknown for many years. It was only a month before the State entry that, in a letter to the Secretary of State, I mentioned as a source of personal satisfaction that during the long tour I was then making it was the first undertaken by a Viceroy for ten years that no detectives nor any special police precautions had been necessary, and that seditious agitation was dead.

On arrival at the railway station at Delhi I was met by all the Ruling Princes of the Punjab and received an address of welcome from the Municipality. Outside the station my wife and I mounted the biggest elephant I have ever seen, carrying a silver howdah and wearing the most gorgeous trappings, and a long procession of elephants was formed with all the Ruling Princes on their State elephants, the Government of India, the Headquarter Staff and my own staff, all on elephants. It was a perfect morning and the procession of elephants made a most striking picture of Oriental colour and splendour. We passed through the Queen's gardens, from which the public had been excluded. It was there that I had an unaccountable presentiment of evil and said to my wife, " I feel quite miserable, I am sure something dreadful is going to happen." She replied, " It is only that you are tired and you always dislike ceremonial." Nevertheless, I persisted in my statement. A few moments later the procession entered the Chandni Chowk, the principal street of Delhi, which was packed with people, and I was greeted with the greatest enthusiasm, the cheering being quite deafening. I had not proceeded more than about 300 yards before there was a shattering explosion. My elephant stopped. There was dead silence. My helmet was on the road. I glanced at my wife, saw at once that she was all right, turned to look at the back of the howdah where I saw some yellow powder and remarked, " I am afraid that was a bomb." My wife asked me if I was hurt and I replied that I felt as though somebody had hit me very hard in the back and had poured boiling water over me. The Chief of Police handed up my helmet on the top of a lance and asked for orders. I said the procession was to proceed as before. Wild cheering broke out on all sides, but when the procession had gone a short distance my wife looking behind saw that I was badly wounded and that the servant who had been standing behind me holding the State umbrella was dead and that his body was entangled in the ropes of the howdah. She told me about the dead man and I stopped the elephant at once. While the poor man's body was being removed I fainted from loss of blood and on recovering consciousness found myself lying on the pavement and receiving first aid. I heard afterwards that the elephant being too frightened by the bomb to kneel, it had been necessary to pile up wooden cases and that my A.D.C., Hugh Fraser, had lifted me down like a baby. He was a very strong man. I gave orders that everything was to be carried out as arranged and gave the text of the speech I had prepared to be read at the ceremony by the senior member of my council. This was done, my wish being that India should realize that nothing could deflect the British Government and the Government of India from their declared intention,

I was taken back to Viceregal Lodge in a motor-car in an un-conscious state.

I remembered afterwards that my Indian personal servant, who had been with me shooting on the previous day and who apparently had put on his scarlet uniform over his khaki shooting kit to keep him warm, had also been on the elephant standing behind Winifred, and that after the explosion I had seen him getting off the elephant in khaki and not in uniform. I said to him, " What the devil do you mean by being here in khaki ? " But I learnt afterwards that the explosion had literally blown his uniform to shreds and that he was covered with 30 or 40 minor wounds. He did not hear what I said as the drums of his ears were burst, as was one of mine. Mine healed, but he, poor man, was always deaf afterwards. I secured for him a double pension.

A curious fact is that the explosion of the bomb was so loud and crashing that it was heard six miles away, and yet neither Winifred nor I heard anything ! I suppose our hearing was paralysed by the bomb before the sound could be heard.

The news of this outrage evoked a wave of indignation throughout all classes in India and of sympathy with my wife and me. Nothing could have been more spontaneous and impressive than the thousands of telegrams and resolutions of loyalty and sympathy that poured into Viceregal Lodge from every authority and community in India. I remember, two days after the incident when I was capable of grasping all that it might mean, discussing it with my wife, and in my weakness I literally wept with disappointment, feeling that all the improvement that I had noted in the general situation had disappeared through the wanton act of the miscreants who had planned it. She consoled me and with remarkable foresight expressed the conviction that once I had recovered from my wounds nothing but good would come from it, and that I would have no more trouble from the people of India who would give me the most loyal support. She was perfectly right, and Gokhale, the leader of the opposition in the Legislative Assembly, told my Private Secretary a few months later that he and his party would never oppose me in any measure that I might consider necessary, and he never did. At the same time in reply to a message that I received I announced that my policy in India would not deviate a hair's breadth on account of the attempt on my life. This provoked general satisfaction throughout India, for to the Oriental mind retaliatory measures are justified and even expected. More than one Indian Maharaja praised my self-restraint in not having ordered the troops of my escort to attack the crowd, this being, as one said to me, the procedure to which Delhi was accustomed from the time of the Moguls.

The courage displayed by my wife throughout the ordeal was a theme of praise and wonder in all European and Indian households and it was a source of great pleasure to all in India when reference was made to her fortitude in terms of warm admiration in the King's Speech at the following opening of Parliament in London. I believe this is the only instance of a lady not of royal blood being mentioned by name in a speech from the Throne.

My wounds, which were very painful, took a long time to heal as several small operations were necessary to remove particles of the bomb with which were screws, nails, gramophone needles, etc., but I was determined to open the first meeting of the Legislative Assembly in the new capital which took place ten weeks after the State entry. I was quite unfit to do so, as I had to leave my bed to go to the Chamber. I received a tremendous welcome not only from the members but from the galleries which were packed, which quite upset me by its genuineness. After a short rest I addressed the Assembly for about fifteen minutes and after listening to a few speeches from the leaders, I was given a great ovation on leaving. I returned to bed and two days later went to Dehra Dun for a month.

Two incidents of interest occurred on the journey, one of them being apparent only some months later. The first was that a wild elephant stood on the railway track and for some time refused to move, threatening to attack the engine. The second was that when driving in a car from the station to my bungalow, I passed an Indian standing in front of the gate of his house with several others, all of whom were very demonstrative in their salaams. On my inquiring who these people might be I was told that the principal Indian there had presided two days before at a public meeting at Dehra Dun and had proposed and carried a vote of condolence with me on account of the attack on my life. It was proved later that it was this identical Indian who threw the bomb at me !

In the meantime my council were carrying on the business of government, though I maintained indirect control by keeping in close touch with the Secretary of State by private telegrams.

It was two months after the bomb incident that Crewe telegraphed privately to my wife at the instance of the Prime Minister suggesting that I should come home for six months so as to recover completely my health. It was a very kind action, but, though I was very feeble and still very ill with neuritis and deafness from a broken drum in my ear, after consultation with my wife, I declined the offer, saying that if I had not recovered sufficiently in six months' time I would reconsider it and then decide whether I was fit ever to return. I had so many irons in the fire and so many projects in hand that I wished to bring to a successful issue, that I felt that only under the very sternest necessity could I entrust their handling for six months to a locum-tenens. Moreover, I did not wish my would-be assassins to realize that they had so far succeeded by compelling me to relinquish even temporarily my office. In six months' time my health was entirely restored, but in the meantime, although I took the opportunity of going to Delhi for ten days, so that I should be seen by people, all sorts of rumours were prevalent as to the collapse of my health, and undoubtedly I was still very feeble. Consequently on my return to Dehra Dun I decided that the only way to put an end to these rumours was to go out and shoot a tiger ! This I did to the surprise of many, but very nearly failed owing to my being only just able to get in my shot before the next rifle on my left, and I killed the tiger dead with one shot. Nothing more was heard of my failing health !

One of the most touching results of the attempt on my life at Delhi was that I received from Indians all over India various offerings amounting to about £12,000 as thank offerings for my recovery, to be spent in any way that I might think best. I funded the amount and created a trust by which all sick children in hospitals all over India would every year on my birthday have a little fête and receive a little present.

My first birthday after my recovery, June 20th, was made a day of rejoicing all over India, of which people said there had never been the parallel there. Everywhere children were fêted by Indians at their own expense, many millions being entertained. I myself received no less than 2,400 telegrams and countless letters from various Indian bodies and associations congratulating me and telling me what they were doing for the children to celebrate my birthday and recovery. It was a most satisfactory demonstration of friendliness.

It was in the spring of 1913 that for the first time in the history of India a conference was convoked of Ruling Chiefs at Delhi to discuss the question of the education of their sons and the sons of the Indian aristocracy, and I opened the conference with a short speech. My intention was to draw the Chiefs nearer to the Viceroy by inaugurating an annual informal conference between them, which answered so well that it was followed up each year, and has now developed into a recognized part of the machinery of the Government of India as the Chamber of Princes.

Everything was quiet and peaceful in the spring and early summer of 1913 except in eastern Bengal, where dacoities were prevalent, committed by educated youths upon their own countrymen, and with which the Government of Bengal seemed to be quite unable to cope. To meet this situation I sent two

battalions of infantry to assist the police and arranged that
divisional manœuvres should take place in eastern Bengal after
the rains with a good show of British troops and artillery. The
population was duly impressed and this measure completely
successful. I have been told that this demonstration is still
remembered for the excellent impression it made.

The representative of the Labour Party on the Islington
Commission, which sat in India in the cold weather of 1912–13
to inquire into the organization of the Indian Civil Service, was
Mr. Ramsay MacDonald, whom I entertained at Delhi with the
other members of the Commission, and who seemed particularly
friendlily disposed towards me. Nevertheless, his stay in India
coincided with the first serious railway strike there had ever
been in India. It broke out immediately after his departure.
The Government of India grasped the nettle and gave orders
for the immediate dismissal of all strikers, and Royal Engineers
were employed in their places with complete success. The strike
was not based upon any grievances of the men but simply upon
the desire of a sort of trade union or association of railway men
to obtain recognition from the Government as the medium of
communication with the men. Had we yielded we should
have been at the mercy of the association. The idea of the
strikers had been to paralyse the railway between Bombay and
Madras. The strike was a complete failure, and after several
weeks of much suffering the strikers begged to be reinstated
unconditionally. The difficulty was how to do this without
a sign of weakness until somebody suggested that the occasion
of my birthday would be suitable for this reinstatement as an act
of clemency, and this was done, to the relief of everybody
concerned.

Owing to the serious illness of Sir O'Moore Creagh, the
Commander-in-Chief, and his determination to resign in
March 1914, the question of the appointment of his successor
gave me much anxiety. It was the turn for a General of
the British Army to be appointed, and the name of a very

distinguished one was proposed to me, but I felt that in this instance it was necessary to put the established rule on one side and to appoint Sir Beauchamp Duff, of the Indian Army, who had been Lord Kitchener's Chief of the General Staff, and who had a reputation for great administrative ability. After endless pressure I succeeded in obtaining his appointment and he took up his post in 1914 a few months before the outbreak of war. Never was there so great a failure, followed by a most tragic ending. Curiously enough, he was the victim of Kitchener's misguided system of the concentration of everything military in the hands of the Commander-in-Chief, which brought about the recall of Curzon from India in 1905, and which proved to be an impracticable system under the stress of war.

During the summer I received a series of visits at Simla from Ruling Princes and Governors of Provinces. I think the most interesting was that of the Maharana of Udaipur, who had never been to Simla before. He left 500 armed wild men at the foot of the hills as they were not allowed to come to Simla. As descendant of the Sun he is regarded as a sort of deity by the Hindus, and all the leaders of the Hindu community in Simla came to meet him at the station. On his arrival he deigned to speak only to the A.D.C. whom I had sent to meet him, treating all the Hindus with the utmost contempt and not even looking at them. Next morning I sent a carriage to fetch him to see me and he made the two officers who accompanied him run by the side of the carriage, with the result that they collapsed when they reached Viceregal Lodge.

The late Maharaja of Gwalior was one of my most frequent visitors and greatest friends, and his visits were always looked forward to by my daughter. Scindia loved practical jokes and Diamond revelled in playing them on him. During his visits I never quite knew what was going to happen, as there were many surprises which were always amusing without hurting anybody.

During the whole of the year there had been a certain effer-

The Viceroy's Durbar at Gwalior

vescence amongst the Mahomedan population owing to the Turco-Italian war in Tripoli and the war in the Balkans, and this unfortunately came to a head in Cawnpore from the trivial incident of the removal of a small building outside a mosque with a view to widening the street. It resulted in a serious riot in which 16 persons were killed by the armed police, 30 wounded and over 100 arrested. The Lieutenant-Governor, Sir James Meston, proceeded to Cawnpore and restored order, but when I heard the facts I urged him strongly to settle the question of the building once and for all, so that there should be no further cause for trouble. The rioters were of course brought up for trial and this gave rise to a general simmering amongst the Mahomedans in India, who were being gradually worked up by the press while no solution of the building problem was offered by the Government of the United Provinces. The agitation spread slowly all over India and gradually developed into an Imperial rather than a provincial grievance. In the meantime, Sir J. Meston, the Lieutenant-Governor, went on leave to England. When ten weeks had elapsed without any solution I determined to take the matter into my own hands and proceeded by train from Simla to Cawnpore. I reached the city in the morning in the hottest weather. I visited the mosque and after discussing the situation with the Government officials, the police officers and leaders of the Mahomedans on the spot, I arrived at what seemed to me to be a possible compromise. I then received a deputation from the Mahomedan community and gave the terms of my proposed compromise, which they readily accepted. Later in the day I called a general meeting of the whole of the Mahomedan community and made them a speech in which I told them that I was their father and they were my children and as such I had the right to say what I liked to them and even to chastise them if necessary. This sentiment was received with shouts of applause. I then reproached them severely for their conduct and at its close announced that with a view to closing the incident I gave a free pardon and ordered the immediate release of 106 rioters. My speech and act of clemency were received not only in Cawnpore but throughout India with the greatest enthusiasm. Telegrams of gratitude poured in from Mahomedan communities and the agitation died as quickly as it had arisen. In discussing the speech I was going to make I told my Private Secretary how I intended to address the Mahomedans as my children. He tried to dissuade me, saying that it would not be understood. From my experience of Mahomedan psychology I persisted and when I commenced my speech with those words I knew how right I had been. My words were afterwards quoted everywhere in the press as evidence of my fatherly solicitude ! I really believe that the solution of this difficult question was one of the principal contributory causes of the loyal and enthusiastic attitude of Indian public opinion on the outbreak of war a year later.

The Duchess of Aosta, whom I had known formerly when travelling in Italy with King Edward, came to India and I arranged a shooting expedition for Her Royal Highness in which she succeeded in killing a tiger. Her enthusiasm went so far as to have some tiger flesh cooked and to eat it ! It must have been very nasty, as nothing smells worse than a dead tiger.

Public opinion was at one time torn by the news that Maud Allen was coming to dance at Calcutta. I was pressed by the European community to prevent her entry into India, but the objections of the Europeans to some of her dances as being unsuitable for Indians to see induced her to modify her clothes and dances to such an extent that when she came even the Europeans considered them dull and uninteresting. Anyhow, I gave full marks to Maud Allen for her behaviour.

Immediately after my visit to Cawnpore I paid a State visit to Kapurthala. I went without my wife, ostensibly owing to the presence of the Maharani who had been a Spanish dancer, but really owing to information received from the secret police of the likelihood of a bomb being thrown at me on my arrival. It was very uncomfortable, but as a precaution I took with me

my own State carriages and horses and my own escort and had
the Maharaja to sit beside me in my carriage. The visit passed
off without the occurrence of any untoward incident, but I
confess to having been anxious when I passed the actual place
from which I had been told the bomb would probably be thrown.
I inquired afterwards if anything had happened to change the
mind of the bomb-thrower, and I was told that two hours before
my arrival a message had been received from the head of the
anarchists telling his accomplices to do nothing " as the Viceroy
had suffered so much this 'year". The working of the Hindu
mind is really beyond anybody's comprehension !

This was the beginning of my autumn tour of a very strenuous
nature, in which I visited Bikaner, Hyderabad, Mysore, Ajmer,
Bangalore, Kolar goldfields, Madras, Patna and Calcutta after
a very short stay in Delhi. Even before starting I received
notice of no less than thirty-seven addresses that were to be
presented to me, to each of which I had to reply in a prepared
speech.

At Bikaner I had a delightful time as usual with wonderful
sport amongst the black buck. The Maharaja, besides being a
first-rate sportsman, was one of the best shots with a rifle that I
have ever seen. My visit to Hyderabad was satisfactory and I
had an interesting exhibition of cheetah hunting bucks. A buck
really does not stand a chance against a cheetah, but what is
curious is that the cheetah always goes for the biggest buck in
the herd and never for a doe.

My visit to Mysore was one of the most interesting visits I
made. The moment one enters the State of Mysore one cannot
help realizing that there is an older and more advanced form of
civilization than elsewhere in India, this being undoubtedly due
to the fact that Madras was the first point of British penetration
into India and that the State of Mysore was for fifty years
administered by the British. The administration of the State is
better than any other, while the Maharaja is one of the best and
most respected in India. He and his brother were very good

89

racquets players and there is a very good racquets court in the Palace. The Maharaja and his brother challenged my staff, being unaware that amongst them there were two of the best racquets players in England. The result was a surprise.

The Maharaja took me out three or four times after bison and I managed to secure two splendid bulls, but it was very hard work. He also organized a *keddah*, when a large number of wild elephants were corralled in a stockade and finally led away into captivity. It was a wonderful sight to see hundreds of elephants crossing a broad river, amongst them being two female elephants supporting a baby elephant with their trunks, and finally being manœuvred by tame elephants into the stockade where they were eventually secured. I felt rather sad at seeing a magnificent old elephant, said to be about 70 years of age, making such a splendid fight inside the stockade that he had to be led away by five tame elephants to his place of captivity, which he soon demolished. The poor animal died shortly afterwards of a broken heart !

We lived in a charming camp near the scene of the *keddah*, and the Maharaja of Gwalior was in another camp alongside. Soon after our arrival he came and asked me if he might have his meals with us in our camp. I said of course that we would be delighted, but asked why he did not feed with our host the Maharaja of Mysore. He replied that the Maharaja was of such high caste that he had his meals alone. I found afterwards that this was true.

We visited also Seringapatam and the Kolar goldfields where within the space of two hours I saw the whole process of auriferous stones being brought up from the mine to the surface, crushed and finally an ingot of pure gold extracted from them. I was told I could take the ingot if I could lift it !

From Mysore we went to Madras, where a speech that I made caused considerable excitement. For three years previously India had been singularly patient over the unfair treatment of Indians in South Africa by the Union Government, and the protests of the Government of India had been practically ignored both by the Dominions Office at home and the Union Government, who seemed to regard India as a negligible quantity. Harassed by invidious and unjust laws, the Indians in South Africa had taken matters into their own hands by organizing passive resistance to these laws. The South African authorities adopted retaliatory measures and reports reached India of the flogging of passive resisters and strikers, and their imprisonment in the mines. The result was that a flame of protest and resentment broke out all over India and the situation was becoming extremely grave. Some people said that there had been no movement like it since the Mutiny. I must say I was personally exasperated at the action of the Union Government and the inaction of the Dominions Office, and this feeling came to boiling-point as I read, while in the train on my way to Madras, the official telegrams recounting the sufferings of the Indians in South Africa. Consequently on arrival at Madras where I had to receive twelve deputations from various bodies in the presence of some thousands of people, I explained fully in a speech the action taken by the Government of India to secure justice in the treatment of Indians in South Africa, and referring to the attitude of passive resistance adopted by the Indians. I said, " In all this they have the sympathy of India—deep and burning and not only of India but of all those who, like myself, without being Indians themselves, have feelings of sympathy for the people of this country." These words were cheered with frenzy and my speech had a magic effect. The agitation ceased at once, since the people had immediate confidence in me and my Government, while I on the other hand felt that the Government of India had the whole of India behind them.

My speech produced a storm in South Africa which had its repercussion in London. Generals Botha and Smuts pressed for my recall. I was asked by the Home Government for explanations and I repeated what I had said as being justified by events and pressed for the appointment of a Commission of Inquiry in South Africa. I was quite unrepentant. The question of my recall was seriously discussed by the Cabinet, but in the end they realized that it would be impossible to recall me in view of what the feeling in India would be. In any case, my action and attitude were entirely justified by the fact that the Union Government were forced by public opinion to appoint a Commission of Inquiry, to which I deputed Sir Benjamin Robertson, Chief Commissioner of the Central Provinces, to attend as representative of the Government of India, and within the space of a few months the unfair laws were modified to the satisfaction of the Indians in South Africa.

An interesting sequel to the above is that when I met Generals Botha and Smuts at the Peace Conference in Paris we discussed this question and I asked General Botha what he would have done in my place. He replied that he would have done the same but in much stronger language !

From Madras I went to Patna, the capital of the new province I had created, where I received a very enthusiastic welcome, inspected the new buildings of the capital and laid the foundation-stone of the new Courts of Justice. After a short stay I went on to Calcutta on a visit to the Governor, Lord Carmichael. I was received in a friendly spirit by the European community, but the precautions taken for my safety were so preposterous and ridiculous that had I known their extent I would not have gone to Calcutta.

There was one incident that pleased me intensely as it was so unexpected. Four of my A.D.C.s asked permission to precede me to Calcutta and to enter for the All-India Polo Championship Tournament. Of course I agreed, thinking it was very sporting of them but that their chance of winning was nil. Although they had a very limited number of quite ordinary ponies, to my great surprise they won every match and finally in a great struggle just won the cup. They had defeated all the regimental teams and polo clubs and had established a record. I was very proud of them and felt a secret satisfaction in swooping down on Calcutta from Delhi and carrying off this greatly prized trophy.

Shortly after my return to Delhi from Calcutta I paid a visit to Sir James Meston at Lucknow, and went for four days into camp in the Kerri jungles. We had very good sport, our bag consisting of 14 swamp deer, three panthers and some smaller game. I took the Maharaja of Bikaner with me as my guest. Meston and his wife were very agreeable hosts and we enjoyed our stay with them.

Just at this time a very tiresome question arose which might have become acute. Sir J. Jordan, Minister in China, moved by missionary opinion, urged upon Sir E. Grey the desirability of the Government of India buying back from the Chinese Government the opium which had been legitimately sold to them the previous year. The minimum cost of this purchase would have been three millions sterling. As the Government of India had already renounced all further export of opium to China, thus entailing a loss of revenue of four millions sterling per annum, this would have been the last straw to break the camel's back. Sir E. Grey, who was always influenced to a certain extent by Exeter Hall, supported the suggestion that the opium sold under treaty to China should be reshipped to India and compensation given to the dealers. The Government of India resisted to their very utmost this injustice to India, and I gave it clearly to be understood that in the event of the Government of India being ordered by His Majesty's Government to pay compensation to the opium merchants in China I would feel it my duty to send in my resignation as Viceroy. Happily the Cabinet came finally to the conclusion that the attitude of the Government of India was irresistible and the question was allowed to drop.

In February 1914 we paid a State visit to Jodhpur to the young Maharaja, who had just returned from school at Wellington College and had been placed upon the *gaddi* by his uncle, the venerable Sir Pertab Singh. He seemed such a nice boy and told me that what he had liked at Wellington College was that if he hit anybody he was hit back at once, and that he missed getting hits of that kind in his own State. He also told me that he had thoroughly enjoyed pawning a pair of boots for a few shillings to spend in the school tuck-shop. It is sad to relate that this charming boy died of drink in a few years' time just as his father had died before him.

It was very inspiriting to see all the young princes and Rajput Sirdars turned out every morning at 6 a.m. by old Sir Pertab, aged 70, and made to go through physical exercises, riding and practising polo for a couple of hours. There was no grumbling and they did it all in a most sportsmanlike manner. The Rajputs of Jodhpur were a very fine lot.

Having by March 1914 spent 3½ years in India, we decided that my wife should go to England for six months for a complete change and much-needed rest, returning to India in the autumn in time for my autumn tour. We therefore went to Bombay on the 20th March and received a most enthusiastic reception in that city. When an address was presented to me by the Corporation in the Town Hall it was several minutes before I could reply owing to the cheering, and the same when I opened the Victoria Docks, the finest in India, on the following morning. This was the last public function that I performed in India accompanied by my wife. In the afternoon I accompanied her on board ship and then said good-bye to her. It was a sad moment for me, but I did not then know how sad. I returned to Government House and from Malabar point watched her ship fading slowly in the distance and in the evening gloom. I never saw her again. I returned immediately to Delhi to wind up the legislative session.

From Delhi I went to Gwalior for a tiger-shooting expedition to last a fortnight, and we had the most marvellous sport, the bag being 24 tigers and two bears, of which I shot 14 tigers and one bear. On one occasion we came across 10 tigers in one valley, of which we killed eight, really in about a quarter of an hour. When we first got to the ground they seemed to me to be running about like rabbits ! The valley having plenty of

THEIR EXCELLENCIES ON TOUR, 1913

water and shade was surrounded by desert and had not been disturbed for years. I shot three of the eight.

The Maharaja of Rewah having pressed me to pay him a visit I went there from Gwalior. Rewah is a backward state and the Maharaja, though very friendly and loyal, was uncultured but a renowned sportsman. What amused me greatly was that on my first day there he took me out after bison which were driven, but the drive turned out badly and I did not get a shot. Nevertheless he presented me with a fine stuffed head of a bison which I suspected he had intended to present to me as the head of the bison I had shot if I had had the chance of letting off my rifle. On the following day to show his skill as a sportsman he had three simultaneous and different drives conducted entirely by himself from an elephant in which there were three separate tigers, and he brought them all up to within 100 yards of me and within a quarter of an hour. Happily I shot them all, which pleased him greatly. There was, however, another occasion when he was not so pleased. He was conducting a drive and pushing up a tiger towards me when a cheetah dashed out from the jungle and I shot it. It was of far greater interest to me as I had never seen a wild one, but the Maharaja was disappointed all the same. While staying with him I expressed a wish to see his son and heir, who was kept in a palace miles away from him. I asked the reason for this and he replied that it was because all sons wished to poison their fathers and that his son was thus removed from temptation ! When he came to see me he proved to be a charming, good-looking boy of 14. I should here add that on the outbreak of war six months later this splendid sportsman offered me all the resources of his State and even all his jewellery, which was very considerable.

From Rewah I went with Diamond to Dehra Dun and then straight to Simla, stopping for one night at Sabathu to present new colours to the Northumberland Fusiliers. It was an interesting ceremony but, though in the hills, Sabathu is a terribly hot place and the day and early morning were rendered hideous by the shrieking of an immense number of brain-fever birds. Diamond and I were quite glad to leave for Simla. That battalion was one of the first to go to the war and I believe every officer who was at Sabathu was killed by the end of the war.

I was very fully occupied during the months of May, June and July in handling the situation in Bengal in connection with proposals for a new Surveillance Bill so as to cope with the un-, rest and the dacoities that were prevalent and which Carmichael and his Government appeared to be quite impotent to control. My own views were in favour of using widely the power of arbitrary arrest and deportation under Regulation 3 of 1818, but the Cabinet in London were not much in favour of this. However, the Bill died a natural death since after the outbreak of war much more stringent measures were available to meet the situation.

Another preoccupation at this time was the architects' plans for Delhi. I had no trouble with Baker,[1] whose plans were admirable and within the figure prescribed for the estimate, but Lutyens' plans, though beautiful, were made absolutely regardless of cost and had to be reduced in every way, which created some unpleasantness. He told people, the Queen amongst them, that I had quite spoilt his plans, but I think I was generous in allotting to him more than half a million sterling to build Government House.

An amusing incident typical of India occurred during this summer. There was to be a horse-show at Simla, and Captain Benson, one of my A.D.C.s, was running it. One day he left 4,000 rupees upon his table in the A.D.C.s' room, and when he returned a few minutes later the money had disappeared, and it was proved that nobody had been into the room except native servants. He naturally made a fuss, but without result. It was then suggested to him that he should invoke the aid of a sooth-sayer, and though sceptical he followed this advice. A sooth-

[1] Sir Herbert Baker associated with Sir Edwin Lutyens in the architecture of New Delhi.

sayer was found and he was promised good payment if the money was recovered. The soothsayer had a private meeting with all the servants, more than 500, and threatened them with all sorts of pains and penalties if the thief did not confess and surrender the money. He said that he knew who the thief was. As the next day nothing had happened the soothsayer summoned another meeting of the servants, when he would, he said, point out the thief and hand him over for punishment, but before the hour of the meeting, Captain Benson found the money put back on the very table from which it had been taken. It was quite clear that the servants really thought that the soothsayer had the power of knowing who was the thief and my personal opinion was that a number of the servants did actually know who had taken the money.

It was about this time that an agitation began throughout India to press for the extension of my office as Viceroy for an additional two years, but it received no encouragement from me, as I had already had an exceptionally hard time during the 3½ years I had spent in India, and I felt that the usual term of five years was as much as my strength would stand. I little realized then what a tremendous strain for another two years was before me owing to the outbreak of war a few months later and the request of the Government that I should remain in India for an additional six months.

Early in July 1914 my wedded life of twenty-four years was broken by the death of my wife in London after a short and unexpected illness. I was entirely knocked out by this blow and was only saved from collapse by the untiring kindness and sympathy of Diamond, then only 14 years old, and by the pressure of work due to the outbreak of war three weeks later. I need hardly say that the whole of India sorrowed for her whom they adored, and overflowed with sympathy for me.

CHAPTER VII

WAR, 1914

IT was only six days before the outbreak of war on August 4th that I was warned officially of the probable imminence of war. Every preparation was immediately made, and I was greatly interested in supervising the application of the regulations which a strong interdepartmental committee, of which I was chairman, had formulated to be carried out on the outbreak of war and which I had signed a few days before I left London for India. Under these regulations every precaution was taken against destructive acts by Germans and Austrians in India, and a large number of German and Austrian ships were seized in Indian ports. Unfortunately, owing to doubt as to the attitude of Austria, I received orders from home to release the Austrian ships, and those that could get away sailed for the Dutch East Indies. We were, however, able to retain a considerable number that were not ready to sail and in a few days war was declared against Austria and the capture of these ships was made effective. As an interesting detail I may mention that I, as Viceroy of India, signed a declaration of war by India against Germany and Austria.

The outbreak of war against Germany met with a very patriotic response from public opinion in India. It was fully realized that the struggle was one for the liberty of Europe and against the military domination of Germany with all the results that a successful war against the Allies would entail as affecting Britain's Dominions and Dependencies. Support was promised on every side and the war measures and precautions taken by the Government of India were never questioned or obstructed. India as a whole was determined to throw her full weight into the struggle and to prove her absolute solidarity with the British Empire. In all my speeches I explained what had been for some time the inevitability of war and the absolute necessity of presenting a solid and united front in defence of the Empire, and I expressed my confidence in the people of India and that, in denuding the country of troops which would proceed to the seat of war, the people themselves would see that peace reigned at home in India so that nothing should deflect the Government from its purpose to assist materially in securing victory wherever British Indian troops might be employed. My confidence was fully justified, since during the twenty months of war that elapsed while I was still in India, there were no serious disturbances and merely a few isolated plots, mostly instigated from outside India, and the people showed themselves to be thoroughly patriotic and loyal. The sentiment of mutual confidence and co-operation that prevailed was indeed inspiring.

It is very difficult to describe the course of the war, as far as India was concerned, and the effort made by India in every quarter where war was in progress. I will try to recall the most salient features of India's effort during the twenty months of war which included the concluding period of my Viceroyalty.

Immediately on the outbreak of war India offered the Home Government two complete divisions of infantry and one division of cavalry for service overseas, with one division of infantry in reserve. These were readily accepted and immediately mobilized and despatched as soon as the requisite transports were available. They were ordered to proceed to Egypt, Malta and Gibraltar, but I protested vigorously and demanded that these splendid divisions should be sent to France, pointing out the slur that would be imposed on India by the presence of Algerian and Senegalese troops in the French Army in France, and that the patriotic enthusiasm for the war in India would receive a serious damper if the activities of the Indian divisions were restricted to garrison duties in the Mediterranean. After some pressure my view was accepted by the Cabinet and these fine divisions arrived in France just in time to fill a gap in the British line that could not otherwise have been filled.

In spite of the severity of the weather and of their unfamiliar surroundings they behaved with great gallantry but suffered terrible losses in the trenches. I had previously succeeded in obtaining the right of Indian soldiers to receive the Victoria Cross for bravery and they won two Victoria Crosses within their first month in France. Very few survived to return to India. It was curious that the two Gharwali battalions composed of men who must originally have been a cross strain between Rajputs and Ghurkas, and who were rather looked down upon in the Indian Army, fought the best. They earned the first Indian V.C. Only fifty men survived of the two battalions and they came to General Willcocks and asked that they might be allowed to return to India in order that their own people might know what they had done. The General supported the request, but it was refused by a higher authority, who did not understand or sympathize with Indian sentiment. In order to recognize the bravery of these two battalions I inquired of the inhabitants of the Gharwal Mountain what they would like me to give them. To my surprise they replied that they would like a seat to be given them in the Legislative Assembly of the United Provinces. I arranged that for them, but as I learnt that lawyers were trying to secure the seat I made the condition that it should always be held by an ex-officer of the Indian Army.

Simultaneously with the despatch of troops to France I ordered the mobilization of three divisions on the Afghan frontier as I anticipated serious danger from the tribesmen in this direction. I had always succeeded in maintaining friendly relations with the Ameer of Afghanistan, with whom I was in constant friendly correspondence, but I realized that with the outbreak of war in Europe he would be subjected to great pressure from the Mullahs and the tribesmen to seize the opportunity to attack us on the frontier. I would like here to bear witness to the constant loyalty of the Ameer to his promise to me to maintain neutrality, and to his efforts (not always successful) to restrain the tribesmen on his side of the frontier from aggressive action. I always had a high opinion of the statesmanship and independence of the Ameer.

In September a mixed Indian division was sent to East Africa. This expedition was an unfortunate affair in which India held no responsibility. I was told by the India Office that they would run the expedition and that all that I had to do was to provide the troops that they themselves would select for an attack upon German East Africa. I did what I was told but expressed my disapproval of expeditions managed abroad by Government Departments at home, with my knowledge of the failure of such expeditions when run by the Foreign Office in the past in Nigeria, Somaliland, etc., and gave my opinion that it was a mistake to fritter away one's efforts in side-shows, since at the end of a successful war the German colonies would necessarily fall into the hands of the victors. Anyhow, this was not the view of the Government at home. The expedition disembarked at a place called Tanga, where the jungle came down to the sea. The Germans were well prepared, having assembled there in considerable numbers since they had had information of the proposed landing. When the troops advanced after disembarkation they were received with heavy artillery fire, and although our troops succeeded in maintaining themselves in the position they had seized, the expedition resulted in complete failure and considerable loss. One Indian regiment, specially selected by General Sir E. Barrow, ran away at the first shot into the sea, throwing away their arms and accoutrements and swimming for the transports. This happened to be one of the regiments that I regarded as worthless and wished to abolish but failed to do so owing to the obstruction of O'Moore Creagh when Commander-in-Chief.

In October and November two further divisions of infantry and one brigade of cavalry were sent to Egypt, and a regiment of Indian infantry operated with the Japanese in the capture of Tsing-tao from the Germans.

It was at the beginning of November that war was declared

against Turkey. During the first three months of the war the attitude of Turkey inspired much misgiving, but it was very necessary that, owing to the attitude of the Mahomedans in India, no provocation for war should be given. As soon, however, as Turkey, at the instigation of Germany, declared war against the Allies, a force was sent up the Persian Gulf under General Barrett which seized the forts at Fao, at the mouth of the Shatt-el-Arab, and when reinforced to the strength of a division captured and occupied the town of Busra. I only wish we had remained there and never advanced further, since India had by that time been bled white by the War Office, and when India's need became pressing and requests were made for drafts, machine-guns, aeroplanes, bombs, etc., they were in almost every case refused.

Within six months of the outbreak of war seven divisions of infantry and two divisions and two brigades of cavalry were sent from India overseas. But in addition to these organized forces no less than 20 batteries of artillery and 32 battalions of British infantry, 1,000 strong and more, were sent to England. Altogether 80,000 British officers and troops and 210,000 Indian officers and men were sent from India overseas during the first six months of the war. I would here remark that the largest Indian expeditionary force ever previously sent from India overseas amounted to 18,000 men. It is interesting to note as regards the army in India that of nine British cavalry regiments seven were sent overseas, of 52 British infantry battalions 44 went overseas, and of Royal Artillery batteries 43 out of 56 were sent abroad. Twenty out of 39 Indian cavalry regiments and 89 out of 138 Indian infantry battalions were also sent overseas. It is a fact that for several weeks before the arrival of some untrained Territorial battalions from England the total British garrison in India, a country bigger than Europe and with a doubtful factor on the North-West Frontier, was reduced to less than 15,000 men. It was a big risk, but I took it, in spite of the repeated and vigorous protests of the Commander-in-Chief and of some of the European community, as I trusted the people of India in the great emergency that had arisen, and I told them so, and my confidence was not misplaced.

At the outbreak of war India was absolutely ready for war in the light of what was then recognized as the requisite standard of preparation of India's military forces and equipment. The army was at full strength, the magazines were full and the equipment complete. At the same time India supplied England in her need within the first few weeks of the war with 560 British officers of the Indian Army who could ill be spared, 70 million rounds of small-arm ammunition, 60,000 rifles, more than 550 guns of the latest pattern, together with enormous quantities of material such as tents, boots, clothing, saddlery, etc., every effort being made to meet the increasing demands of the War Office. All the Indian aeroplanes with the personnel of the Indian Air Force were sent to England or Egypt, and the later demands of India for aeroplanes in Mesopotamia when the need was great were entirely ignored.

The foregoing is a brief summary of the great military effort made by India at the beginning of the war, but this was almost overshadowed by the splendidly loyal and patriotic response of all the Ruling Princes and Chiefs to the appeal that I addressed to them for their loyal support and assistance. Every one of them without exception offered personal service, troops, hospital ships, money, nurses and all the resources of their States ; one of them, the Maharaja of Rewah, as I have already stated, offering all his personal jewels. A telegram I sent home, recounting their loyal offers, provoked the greatest enthusiasm when read in the two Houses of Parliament. I accepted from them every offer of a practical nature and a large number of them went overseas to the war with their own contingents.

We had many moments of anxiety when large convoys of ships loaded with troops and very inadequately guarded were crossing the Indian Ocean to Aden owing to the very successful raids of the German cruisers *Emden* and *Koenigsberg* which destroyed an enormous amount of British shipping in the Indian Ocean and Bay of Bengal. Had the *Emden* met one of our convoys she could, by the superior range of her guns, have destroyed the convoy and the ships protecting it without any risk to herself. Happily, after a very adventurous career during which she shelled the town of Madras, she was caught by an Australian cruiser and after a very gallant fight was completely destroyed. The *Koenigsberg* was also run to ground in a river on the coast of East Africa and destroyed by aeroplanes.

During these early weeks of the war I had a great personal preoccupation and anxiety. My eldest boy, aged 22, a lieutenant in the 15th Hussars, landed in France on the 15th August with his regiment and went straight up to the front. On the 23rd August he was selected by his Commanding Officer, owing to his good knowledge of French, to make a reconnaissance to discover the movement of a German force which was creating some uneasiness to the British General. He was told to go to a certain village which the German outposts had already reached. Taking five troopers with him, he hid them and their horses just on the outskirts of the village and himself proceeded alone into the village to the house of the *curé*, who took him up into the belfry of the church. He remained there most of the night and was able to discover and report very important movements of German troops. On hearing his troopers exchanging shots with the Germans in the village he quickly rejoined them and returned with what was considered most valuable information. Two days later he, with his troop, numbering thirty-five in all, were sent to disengage a company of the Royal Munster Fusiliers that was surrounded. They succeeded in doing so and killed 145 Germans, but he received several machine-gun wounds in both arms and at the end of the fighting had to retire to an ambulance. For this and the reconnaissance he was immediately recommended for the D.S.O. for exceptional reconnaissance work and gallantry in the field, and received it a few weeks later. The King telegraphed to me that he had conferred it upon him.

For more than a week during the retreat from Mons, he was jolted along bad roads in an ambulance waggon with practically no food and little medical attention until he arrived at St. Nazaire, where at last I heard of him in Lady Dudley's hospital. Some weeks later he was moved to England, and although for some time his wounds were said to be making fairly good progress, so much so that it had been arranged that he should come to me in India, the wounds became gangrenous and the poor boy died at Folkestone in the following December. He was such a splendid boy in every way and I was very proud of him.

In addition to these sorrows I had other causes for sadness. Naturally, all my A.D.C.s wished to rejoin their regiments at the outbreak of war, and of course I agreed to their return to England. There were terrible casualties amongst them. Hugh Fraser and Wisher Forrester were killed on the same day and John Bigge a few days later. Willie Cadogan and Atkinson, who commanded the Bodyguard, were killed a few months later, and later on John Astor lost a leg and Muir was badly wounded in the stomach. Benson and Nicolson were the only two who escaped unscathed. Considering that these had spent most of the four years I had been in India in daily contact with me in my official residence or wherever I might be, they were to me more than ordinary friends, and I felt very deeply their deaths and wounds.

On the other hand, my son Alec joined me shortly after the outbreak of war, and later became one of my A.D.C.s till my return to England, when he joined the Grenadiers and went to the front. A little later, Errington,[1] who had been my Private Secretary both in St. Petersburg and at the Foreign Office, came to me as A.D.C., not being fit enough to go to the front with the Grenadiers, and brought with him his charming wife, Lady Ruby. They were both of them a great help and comfort to me and Diamond.

The only military officer that I retained on my staff was my

[1] Afterwards 2nd Earl of Cromer.

Military Secretary, Colonel Maxwell, V.C., a most gallant officer who applied at once to go to England, but I had to refuse. He could not understand that during the war I had more need of a capable officer at my elbow to help me than at any other time, and there was absolutely nobody else to replace him. It was very unpleasant for me to refuse both him and his wife, who begged me to allow him to go. I told the latter that she ought to thank me, for I knew how reckless he was of danger, and that if he went to the war he would probably soon be killed. He returned with me to England a year and a half later, obtained at once the command of a regiment and shortly afterwards the command of a brigade, fought extraordinarily well, and was killed by a German sniper when reconnoitring alone with an orderly the enemy position in front of his brigade. This was within three months of his going to the front in France. His death was a great sadness to me.

Another officer who behaved very well towards me was General Birdwood, my Official Secretary in the Army Department. About six weeks after the outbreak of war he told me that he had been offered by Kitchener the command of the Australian contingent, but that he realized that India having been bled white of officers, it would be extremely difficult if not impossible for me to find a competent officer to take his place, and that if I said the word he would stick to me and refuse the offer that had been made to him. I told him at once that he had put the question to me in such a way that it was impossible for me to refuse and that he was to accept the appointment. Finally he commanded an Army, became a Field-Marshal and Commander-in-Chief in India. He was a splendid and very loyal officer to me in India.

About three months after the outbreak of war twenty-nine Territorial batteries and thirty-four Territorial battalions were sent to India to replace British troops. They were welcome in the denuded state in which India found herself, but they had to be trained, armed and equipped. Their rifles were no better

than gaspipes, and for clothing they had only what they stood
up in and that had no pretence of fitting. One battalion had 500
unserviceable rifles, all marked " D.P." (drill purposes). As
for the artillery, the guns could not be fired as the breech-
blocks, instead of having fittings of asbestos, had wood painted
to look like asbestos, and the ammunition was marked " Dangerous and not to be used for practice " ! Nevertheless, the men
were very superior and intelligent and after six months' training
with proper guns, rifles and clothes, some of these Territorial
batteries and battalions became very smart and efficient, and
were employed on the frontier and in Mesopotamia. I selected
Lord Suffolk's battery and Lord Radnor's battalion of Territorials
for service in the camp at Delhi. Lord Suffolk's battery was
composed entirely of men from his own estate. It became
extremely efficient and was eventually sent to Mesopotamia
where, to the regret of all, Lord Suffolk, the most perfect
type of English gentleman, was killed in action with his
battery.

In spite of the friendly and loyal attitude of the Ameer of
Afghanistan, in whom I had real confidence, the situation on
the frontier was very disturbed and inspired grave anxiety. In
the first twelve months of the war there were repeated attacks by
Afghan tribesmen on our frontier, but they were handled so
promptly by a specially organized mobile brigade and such
heavy defeats and punishment inflicted upon them that there
was no more trouble afterwards. As an example of the mobility
of this brigade I was informed at 7 a.m. one morning by tele-
phone of an attack on a fortified post at Miranshah. I com-
municated at once with the Commander-in-Chief who sent the
necessary orders, and the whole brigade had moved out by
10 a.m. the same morning. To prevent night raids a fence of
live wire was extended along some parts of the frontier and was
most effective. Counter-measures were taken with the utmost
energy. If ever any tribesmen raided our territory a retaliatory
raid was immediately carried out into tribal territory, their

crops were burnt and their cattle driven off by our troops. They very soon realized that it was not a paying game. A few months later I met some Pathans near Simla who had evidently come to trade in India, and they told me that they had been fighting against our troops in the spring but that they would not fight again as we did not fight fairly any more ! I rather sympathized with the idea of these tribesmen that to fight was a sport in which unfair advantage should not be taken. They said that the use of aeroplanes, armoured cars, bombs and live wires was not playing the game.

It was on the 17th December that I received the sad news of the death of my boy from his wounds. It was not entirely unexpected as I had received some unfavourable telegrams during the two or three preceding days, but the blow was none the less severe. It was overwhelming. India poured out its sympathy in overflowing manner towards me in my sorrow, but nothing could console me for the loss of my wife and eldest son during the short space of six months, to say nothing of the losses in the war of so many members of my staff whom I regarded as almost members of one family. Diamond and I went quietly off to Dehra Dun to spend Christmas and what remained of the saddest year of my life.

I was in Delhi on the 1st January to hold the King's Proclamation Parade, held for the first time in Delhi. It was only remarkable for the number of mounted infantry officers who could not manage their horses. The Legislative Council met a few days later, and having passed such legislation as was necessary adjourned for six weeks.

In the meantime, feeling tired and greatly upset by my sorrows, I obtained permission from the Secretary of State to go to Busra to investigate the political situation in Mesopotamia and to arrange the lines upon which the Vilayet of Busra was to be administered under our guidance. I had arranged that my surviving son, who had gone to England to join up there, should return to me in India, and after joining the reserve of officers, should serve as one of my A.D.C.s. He met me on my arrival in Bombay.

During my stay in Bombay I visited the hospitals of the wounded who had returned from the various fronts. The Indian soldiers were most comfortably housed and looked after in a hospital organized and very well run by Lady Willingdon. Nothing could have been better. She was crazy about mauve as a colour and I was startled to find everything mauve in colour in the hospital ; even the blankets were mauve. The Indians were very pleased and excited at my visiting them, and those who had had legs amputated asked me to give them what they called an " English leg ", which was a kind of cork leg very superior to the wooden leg supplied by the military medical authorities. Of course I gladly promised to give them all, but it was an expensive affair as each leg cost me £20. I was told afterwards that when discharged from hospital these one-legged soldiers returned to their villages, not wearing their cork legs but regarding them as an object of interest to their village and as a sort of heirloom to their families.

I was deeply touched at seeing in this hospital a fine young Indian soldier *in extremis* but quite conscious. He was told who I was. As I stood at his bedside I placed my hand on his forehead, and I shall never forget the smile of happiness that lighted up his face, and I remained with him till he died, smiling. The simple Indian has a most attractive and lovable nature.

After my visit to the wounded at Bombay I initiated a new rule which proved extremely popular. I gave orders that every wounded Indian soldier on disembarking at Bombay should receive 100 rupees in cash (about £6). Hardly any had ever seen 100 rupees before and they returned to their villages as millionaires.

I also visited the hospital where all the wounded British officers were housed, and I was not at all satisfied with the arrangements for their comfort, which compared very un-favourably with the hospital for the Indians. I made a great fuss about it and insisted that electric light should be installed at once, more bathrooms made, better food supplied, and other improvements. On my return some weeks later I made inquiry and found that these changes had been carried out.

CHAPTER VIII

MESOPOTAMIA, 1915

ON the 25th January I embarked at Bombay with my staff on the Royal Indian Marine Ship *Northbrook*, and after six days in the Persian Gulf, passing as close to the northern shore as possible so as to get a view of Hormuz, Lingah, Jask and Bushire, we arrived at Koweit on the 31st January. It was a very pleasant and most interesting journey, as I was able to view at a short distance places so familiar to me by name. All these places lie on a comparatively narrow strip of coast land backed by high barren mountains six to seven thousand feet high. At Lingah we could see the Turkish Consul's residence beflagged for some imaginary Turkish victory. Bushire looked green and cool in the distance.

On the day following my arrival at Koweit, ceremonial visits were received and paid to the Sheikh of Koweit, a blear-eyed old fox, 80 years old, and the Sheikh of Bahrein, who had come from Bahrein to meet me there. I held a Durbar on board the *Northbrook* and invested the Sheikh of Koweit with the K.C.S.I. and the Sheikh of Bahrein with the C.I.E. The Sheikh of Koweit himself ran the only café to be found in the place that was at all fashionable ! Koweit is really a God-forsaken place with mud walls, mud houses, no trees and no fresh water, the latter being brought to the city in tank boats from the Shatt-el-Arab. It is surrounded by sandy desert except where it faces the sea. Its only industry is boat building. My visit exploded the idea prevalent in India and at home for many years that Koweit was a possible port upon which the Germans had cast their eye as the terminus of the Bagdad railway, and to prevent this the British Government had for several years paid £4,000 per annum to the Sheikh for the lease of the foreshore. As a proof of the absurdity

III

of the idea the *Northbrook*, though only 6,000 tons, could not approach within 2½ miles of the foreshore, and although there was deep water for about 200 yards close in to the shore it was impossible to approach except in a small boat owing to the shallows. It seemed to me incredible that with British officers resident on the spot this fallacy had never been exposed, though they admitted that Koweit could never be a port.

From Koweit we went up the Shatt-el-Arab and arrived at Abadan, the works of the Persian Oil Company, on the 2nd February. I went over the oil works which were very extensive and run by 48 Englishmen with 3,000 to 4,000 workmen. The oil was conveyed to the works by means of a pipeline from wells situated 140 miles distant, and 7,000 tons of crude oil were being shipped monthly from Abadan. During the war the Arabs broke the pipeline two or three times, but it was always quickly repaired. I distributed some rewards and a piece of plate to the officials in recognition of their assistance during the advance of the expeditionary force. Later in the day I went farther up the Shatt-el-Arab to its point of junction with the Karun, and made an expedition up the Karun in a launch. It is a pretty river with date groves and nice houses on the banks. It reminded me to a certain extent of the Thames.

The following day we arrived at Busra, but on our way up the river we stopped opposite the palace of the Sheikh of Mohammerah, who came on board the *Northbrook* and whom I invested with the Order of the K.C.S.I. He was the gentleman who, when I was in charge of the Legation in Tehran in 1897, had murdered his father and occupied his throne. I mentioned that I had been in Tehran at the moment of his accession, and the old rascal winced at the thought that I was aware of his evil deeds.

On arrival at Busra I was received with military and naval salutes and the General with his staff and the Naval Authorities came on board the *Northbrook* as well as a deputation from the British community, who presented me with an address. In my

THE VICEROY ARRIVING AT SHAIBA FORT

reply I gave a definite assurance that Busra would in the future be under a more benign administration than in the past.

After their departure I landed and visited the hospitals and talked to the sick and wounded. They all seemed comfortable and cheery, and the hospitals well run. I gave orders that no expense was to be spared to make the men comfortable, and that precautions were to be taken at once to meet the requirements of the hot weather that was approaching. The only thing I saw and did not like was a large tent full of Indians with venereal diseases, and I told General Barrett that steps should have been taken to prevent this. Later in the day I gave a party on board the *Northbrook* to which everybody in Busra was invited.

On the following day, escorted by a squadron of the 23rd Cavalry, I rode out to Shaiba, a fortified outpost in the desert about 10 miles from Busra which had been the scene of considerable fighting with the Turks. I addressed the troops and congratulated them on their successful defence of the post.

Next morning I left the *Northbrook* for the *Lawrence*, a smaller ship, and went up to Kurna, the junction of the Euphrates and the Tigris. I there visited the advanced camp at Mezara under the command of General Dobbie, and rode round the defences, which seemed very well organized. The following morning I went two miles farther up the Tigris to where H.M.S. *Espiegle* was moored. From her deck I could see plainly the Turkish camp at Rotak, about six miles away. A person who was greatly envied was a very young lieutenant in command of a launch named *Miner*, with a small gun on board, who went up the river every morning to within a mile or so of the Turkish position and fired at anything he could see. He prided himself on having made quite a good bag. On one occasion his boat was holed by a shell, but he beached it, patched it up, returned, had it repaired, and was back again firing at the Turks in three days' time. He was having the time of his life.

On my return to Kurna, it being Sunday, I attended parade service almost at the juncture of the two rivers. Curiously enough, the lesson for the day, Sexagesima Sunday, was the third chapter of Genesis, and as Kurna is one of the reputed sites of the Garden of Eden, the Army Chaplain had a splendid opportunity of preaching a sermon full of local interest, which he failed to do. The Tommies had, however, been much more imaginative, for on walking about the village, I saw the names of streets written up, such as " Adam's Alley ", " Eve's Corner ", " Temptation Square ", etc. The one solitary tree (certainly an old one) was named the " Tree of Knowledge ", etc.

From Kurna we went straight to Muscat in the Persian Gulf to visit the Sultan, and arrived there on February 11th. Muscat is a singularly beautiful harbour surrounded by rugged rocks with a towering fort dating from the days of Portuguese supremacy in those waters. It was impossible to land in a boat and I had to be carried ashore in a chair in full uniform which seemed hardly dignified in front of the guard of honour saluting me and which I had to inspect ! The visit went off very well. I had the opportunity of seeing at Muscat the French depôt which had for many years been a source of diplomatic controversy with the French Government, and I could only wonder that any sensible person could have attached the slightest importance to it.

I felt much sympathy for our Consul, a member of the Indian Political Service, who, living in a very hot climate, was able to take exercise only for a few hundred yards round the Consulate owing to the general unrest that prevailed in the city.

From Muscat the *Northbrook* sailed direct for Karachi, and from there I went on to Delhi.

My visit to the Persian Gulf and Busra proved to be of the greatest use. In place of officers of the Indian Political Service whom I met there unable to speak Arabic, I found and appointed officers who could do so. I came into touch with Commanders of Divisions and Brigades and I obtained the transfer of some who evidently were unable to withstand the climate. Finally, and the most important of all, I was able to discover the needs of our troops both British and Indian, and to provide for them.

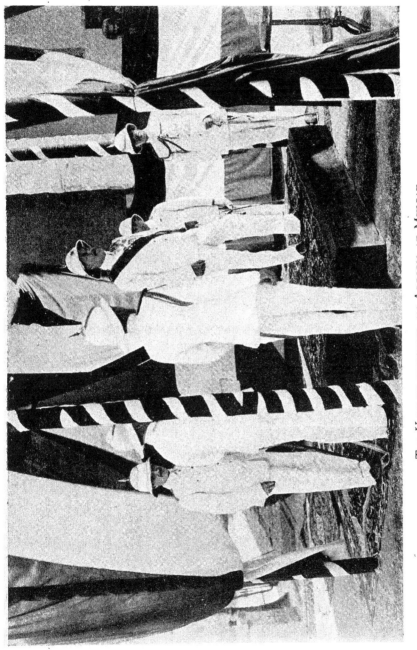

The Viceroy receiving an Address at Muscat

As for myself, it was a most instructive experience and one that
· I shall not forget.

One of the first items of news on my return was the death
of Gokhale. He had been for some time in ill health. He was
. the leader of the Opposition in the Legislative Assembly, a really
good orator and debater, a statesman, and a man for whom I
had the highest respect. He and I worked together very closely
and cordially in our efforts to alleviate the situation of the
Indians in South Africa, and his co-operation was most helpful.
His death was a great loss to India as there was no other statesman
in India of his calibre. He had no illusions as to the necessity
for the maintenance of British rule in India for a great many
years, although he would have liked to see the number of British
officials in India reduced almost to vanishing-point. On one
occasion I said to him, " How would you like it if I were to
tell you that all the British officials and British troops would
leave India within a month ? " He replied, " I would be very
pleased to hear that news, but before you had all reached Aden
we would be telegraphing to you to come back again." His
hostility to Tilak was due to the latter's extremism. It was
shortly after the attack made upon me at Delhi that Gokhale
told Sir James Du Boulay (my private secretary) that I might
rest assured that he would never oppose any measure that I
really wished to be carried in the Legislative Assembly as he
considered that India was heavily in my debt for what had
happened. He was the founder of the " Servants of India
· Society ".

Lord Kitchener having been appointed Secretary of State for
war in August 1914, the post of High Commissioner in Egypt
had been vacant for some months, when I suddenly learnt to my
great surprise that Sir H. MacMahon, who was at home on
leave, had been appointed to succeed him at Cairo. Although
he was Secretary for the Foreign Department I was not consulted.
I learnt that Roos-Keppel had also been suggested for the
post. That would have been a poor appointment, as he was no

administrator, although a first-class frontier officer and quite irreplaceable on the North-West Frontier.

During these months the internal situation began to grow menacing, due to the anarchists realizing our military weakness owing to the depletion of our troops. At this moment the Maharaja of Nepal offered to send me 6,000 troops, an offer that I readily accepted, and 6,000 men were brought very quietly across the frontier to Dehra Dun and Abbotabad, where they were trained by British officers. They were a splendid-looking lot of men, but quite untrained. In less than a year they became absolutely first-class troops, and were gradually drafted to posts on the North-West Frontier. I felt that in those anxious times I had in them a force in reserve that I could use with confidence at any point and against any enemy.

The two provinces of India that created anxiety owing to the unrest that prevailed were Bengal and the Punjab, the former largely owing to the weakness of the Provincial Government, and the latter owing to the arrival and incursion of 700 Sikh revolutionaries from America. The Government of the Punjab succeeded in arresting nearly all the Sikh leaders on their arrival in the province, while the rest who started creating disturbances in the districts were caught by the Sikh villagers and handed over to the police. At the request of Sir Michael O'Dwyer, Lieutenant-Governor of the Punjab, I authorized the seizure and detention in prison, under Regulation III of 1818, of more than 300 Sikh revolutionaries and the police surveillance of a good many more. In view of the situation in the Punjab, and the alarm expressed to me by leading Indians of Calcutta at the prevailing insecurity in Bengal, needing strong executive action, which the Government of Bengal appeared unwilling or unable to take, I decided to introduce a law on the lines of the English Act for the Defence of the Realm, so as to make it easier to cope with crime in those two provinces. This was done and a far more drastic Dora than her English sister, was submitted to the Legislative Assembly. When the Bill was published it provoked a considerable outcry and several Indian members protested to me privately against the stringency of some of its most drastic provisions and said that they would have to oppose the Bill in the Assembly. I told them that they were free to criticize the Bill in debate and to say whatever they pleased against it when it came up for discussion and that I quite appreciated their point of view but that, as responsibility for peace and tranquillity in India rested with me, I nevertheless confidently counted upon them to pass the law in the end. When the Bill came up for debate a large number of amendments were proposed, and the Indian members aired their criticisms freely, but in the end it was passed unanimously with two slight amendments that I accepted when I wound up the debate in a carefully considered speech. Those two trifling amendments " saved the faces " of the Indian critics.

At this stage of the war the recruiting of Indians to fill the vacancies caused by death and wastage in the Indian regiments was going none too well, and especially amongst the Sikhs. There was trouble with the 10th Baluchis, of which the Mahsud Company shot their officer on embarking at Bombay for Mesopotamia. Several of that company were tried and shot, and the regiment was sent in disgrace to Rangoon. There was a good deal of unrest in the Mahomedan native regiments, chiefly due to our war against Turkey.

This Mahomedan fanaticism was largely due to the propaganda of the two brothers Mahomed Ali and Shaukat Ali, leading members of the Khalifat movement, so to put an end to this I interned them in a Hindu village in Central India where they were allowed to go free but under close supervision. The propaganda ceased at once and there was no more trouble in Mahomedan regiments.

Other disturbing incidents took place such as the arrest of a Mahratta anarchist with ten loaded bombs inside the lines of the 12th Cavalry at Meerut where he was in touch with the Sowars, while a conspiracy was discovered to rob the armoury and magazine of certain regiments at Lahore, Pindi and Feroze-pur. The troops were on the look-out for the raiders all night, and on the following morning seven or eight men were caught in Lahore with arms and bombs. All these men were tried by court-martial and given short shrift. Nevertheless, these incidents caused considerable anxiety and uneasiness amongst the European population and great watchfulness was necessary, especially in the cantonments. At the same time I received several warnings from various sources of a projected rising in Bengal within three months.

On the 2nd March 1915 I went with Diamond for three days to Barrackpore, which I had retained as a Viceregal residence. It was rather a long way to go, 1,000 miles there and 1,000 miles back, for so short a visit, but it was necessary and I could not spare more time away from headquarters. On my way there I opened the Sara Bridge over the Hoogly, the largest railway bridge in India, and since named after me. In Calcutta I unveiled the statues of Lord Ripon and Lord Minto which, curiously enough, were quite close to each other on the *maidan*. The two ceremonies were attended by two different crowds of entirely divergent political opinion. I am glad to say I was welcome to both. Lord Ripon's statue was long overdue, but the English community had always refused to have anything to do with it, owing to the Ilbert Bill introduced by Lord Ripon, which was extremely distasteful to English opinion in India, and no subscriptions were forthcoming from English sources. Consequently the statue was paid for entirely by Indians. I was very pleased to unveil the statue as I had known Lord Ripon very well and respected his statesmanship. As Chancellor of Calcutta University I attended the annual convocation and bestowed degrees. I had Lord Carmichael, the Governor of Bengal, and Lady Carmichael to stay with me at Barrackpore, gave a garden party which all Calcutta society were delighted to attend and a large dinner under the famous banyan tree in the garden each of the three evenings that I was there. It is in this manner, at Barrackpore, or as the guest of the Governor in Government House, Calcutta, that, in my opinion, the Viceroy should visit Calcutta, and not as the occupant of Belvedere, a very inferior official residence of the former Lieutenant-Governor of Bengal, and quite overshadowed by Government House, the official residence of the Governor of Bengal.

During the early months of 1915 I had a great many visitors at Delhi, amongst them being the Willingdons from Bombay, the Begum of Bhopal, the Maharaja of Bikaner, the Nawab of Palanpur, and the unexpected visit of the Maharaja of Mysore who had never previously paid a visit to any Viceroy. I very gladly accepted his offer to visit me, but my staff was at once informed that it would be necessary to have a special house built for him to live in with a fixed number of rooms and of a certain size to suit his high-caste principles. Plans were sent of what was required. His food was also to be prepared by his own cooks and to be eaten by him in solitude. I was told that he took his meals on the floor. No furniture was needed for the house ! I realized that his wishes had to be fulfilled to the letter and a house was built for him in the Viceroy's garden of the exact dimensions he required and was ready for him in a month's time. His visit was a great success and he was perfectly charming. I regarded him as a most enlightened ruler and his state as the best administered in India.

The Begum of Bhopal preferred to live during her visit in the State tents provided for distinguished visitors.

After the close of the legislative session I went to Jammu to visit the Maharaja of Kashmir, an old man, but one of the most loyal of the Indian princes. He commenced playing cricket at the age of 63 and had an English cricket professional to teach him. He made his courtiers play, but his innings were interminable as nobody dared to bowl anywhere near the wicket, to hold a catch or to run him out ! I was glad of the opportunity to visit there the wounded Kashmir Imperial Service troops who had returned from East Africa.

During my visit to Mesopotamia in February I came to conclusions on several points. I realized that it was impossible to remain on the defensive at Kurna on the Tigris and at Shaiba in the desert to the south since spies were passing the whole time to and from Busra and the enemy, and the inhabitants were intimidated by false rumours spread by enemy emissaries. It was decided therefore to raise the Mesopotamian force to two complete divisions and to place them under General Nixon, a fine General who had commanded the Southern Army in India. General Barrett was tired and ill and returned home shortly afterwards. He was too old to show initiative and enterprise and had allowed the Turks to settle down and entrench themselves in dangerous proximity to our force at Shaiba.

On Nixon's arrival at Busra he immediately struck a blow at the Turks, and after quite a severe battle he completely routed them and inflicted serious losses. After this battle Nixon, with the approval of the Home Government, advanced to Amara with the intention of holding it as a measure of pacification of the Vilayet of Busra. The capture of Amara was carried out in an exceptional manner, the troops advancing in native boats clad with nothing but their belts and rifles over the flooded land, but the Turks did not wait for them and the Turkish garrison surrendered to fifty soldiers and sailors under the command of General Townshend and Captain Nunn, R.N., on being told that there was a large force behind them. Several thousand prisoners were taken. The advance on Nasryeh was carried on simultaneously and with equal success. The whole of the Vilayet was thus in occupation by our troops and it is a matter for regret that they ever moved farther north. Even in those days the Government of India were doing their utmost to increase their river transport and in addition to steamers bought in India had already bought Thames and Nile steamers, but they all foundered on their way to the Persian Gulf. They would have been perfect for the rivers in Mesopotamia.

It was on the 27th May 1915 that I learnt that my old and

great friend Lord Crewe had resigned on the formation of a Coalition Government and that he was succeeded by Mr. (afterwards Sir) Austen Chamberlain as Secretary of State for India. I received the news with much regret.

There was great annoyance in India when the House of Lords rejected the Bill brought in by the Government for the creation of an Executive Council for the United Provinces. The opposition was led by Lord Curzon and supported by other ex-Viceroys, but it was a foolish step to have taken as only four years later Lord Curzon had, as a member of the Cabinet, to agree to the Montagu-Chelmsford reforms which went a great deal further.

It was at the beginning of June that the Prime Minister made the following announcement in the House of Commons :

" Under normal circumstances Lord Hardinge's term of office as Viceroy and Governor-General of India would have terminated in November next,' but His Majesty's Government, recognizing the great services which Lord Hardinge has rendered to India, and desiring to retain the advantage of his experience during the coming winter, have requested him to remain until the end of March next. Lord Hardinge has readily consented to comply with our wishes and the King has been pleased to approve the arrangement.

." I am glad of the opportunity to express my sense of the public spirit which, in spite of the great strain of his labours, and in face of heavy private sorrows, has led Lord Hardinge to place his services unreservedly at our disposal."

I was instructed by the Home Government to publish this announcement and in doing so I took care to state that it was with no light heart that I had agreed to the prolongation of my onerous responsibilities as Viceroy, but that I had done so in view of the constant and repeated demands of the Ruling Princes and representatives of various communities for the extension of the tenure of my office, and the feeling of the friendly confidence of so many, had given me the courage to continue to fulfil my duties to the best of my ability and for the welfare of India.

After this announcement had been made I was bombarded with letters and telegrams showing that the extension of my office had given general satisfaction throughout India. I had been careful not to show any enthusiasm about it so as to damp down any further demand for a longer extension in the event of war being still prolonged in the spring.

It was not until the following January that I learnt who was to be my successor. In the meantime A. Chamberlain told me that he had submitted four names to Asquith to select from. They were two Earls, a Marquis and a Duke, all of the old Tory type, and Asquith would not look at them. For the sake of decency Chamberlain might at least have included a Liberal peer. I then received instructions to offer the appointment to Lord Chelmsford, who was serving as a Captain in the Territorials, and with his company was guarding the wireless station at Chitogh, near Simla. He ought to have been recalled to England before the offer was made to him as naturally the Indians could not understand how the post of Viceroy could be offered to a Captain of Territorials out in India. He stayed with me for ten days before leaving for England. He was a very nice man, but it remained for India to test his qualities.

It was in June that General Nixon first advocated a move forward from Amara to Kut-el-Amara, but the Government of India turned it down at once. Two months later it was decided with the approval of the Home Government that the advance should be made and this was successfully achieved by General Nixon on the 29th of September.

It was on the 3rd October that General Nixon in a telegram to Austen Chamberlain raised the question of opening the road from Kut to Bagdad, which he said his force was strong enough to do. The Government of India were, however, of the opinion that this could not be safely done without the return from France and the addition to his force of an Indian division. On the 5th October General Nixon sent a further telegram to the Secretary of State urging strongly the advance upon and destruction of a shaken enemy. The Government of India, however, though concurring generally with the views of General Nixon, absolutely refused on the 6th October to allow him to advance beyond Kut-el-Amara without the addition of another division of troops to his force. This decision appeared definitely to limit the activities of General Nixon and his troops. The current of events was, however, changed on the 8th October by an urgent telegram sent direct to General Nixon by Austen Chamberlain inquiring with what force he would be able to occupy and hold Bagdad. Simultaneously I received a telegram from the Secretary of State informing me that the Cabinet were so impressed by the political and military advantages to be obtained by the occupation of Bagdad that they would make every effort to supply the necessary force and asked me whether I was satisfied that one division would suffice. On the same day General Nixon telegraphed to the Secretary of State to the effect that he was confident that he could defeat the Turks and occupy Bagdad without any addition to his actual force, but that in the event of the Turks receiving reinforcements and trying to recapture Bagdad he would require an additional division and one regiment of British cavalry. He added that General Townshend was already at Azizyah, which was halfway to Bagdad.

This telegram following that from the Secretary of State created an entirely new situation. General Nixon was at the head of a victorious army which had fought successful engagements at Shaiba, Amara, Nasryeh and Kut-el-Amara, while General Townshend's division had achieved a reputation of being invincible. The value of such a success as the capture of Bagdad would have been inestimable as a set-off to the failure in the Dardanelles and in maintaining the British position and prestige in Persia, Afghanistan and India. The Government of India had no authority to order the advance to Bagdad. The control of the scope of operations had been laid down as resting in the hands of H.M. Government. The decision, therefore, rested with the latter. Unfortunately it was only four months later that I learnt that, after the battle and capture of Kut, Townshend wrote to Nixon and said that his force was not strong enough to go on to Ctesiphon, but Nixon insisted. Nixon must have been like the proverbial old man in a hurry and anxious to have the credit of taking Bagdad before his health broke down. This correspondence appears amongst the military records. Nixon's responsibility is great.

Bearing in mind the views of the Cabinet upon the " great political and military advantages of the occupation of Bagdad ", the Commander-in-Chief and I came to the conclusion that General Nixon was in the best position to judge as to the number of troops he would require to obtain his objective, and that under the circumstances the Government of India would have placed itself in an invidious position if, at a critical moment during the war, they had overridden the opinion of the General in command in the field and had vetoed the advance to Bagdad.

The question was referred to an interdepartmental committee in London with representatives of the War Office, Admiralty, India Office and Foreign Office, and also by the combined staffs, and the opinion was given that General Nixon's force was adequate to take Bagdad, but that an additional division with some cavalry would be necessary to hold Bagdad, with a second division in readiness as a reserve.

These dates and facts are important as showing the basis upon which the advance to Bagdad was authorized by the Secretary of State on the 23rd October and two divisions were promised as reinforcements " as soon as possible ".

Up to this stage the campaign in Mesopotamia had been an unqualified success and it had been extolled by statesmen at home as one of the most brilliant and successful of the war. Three months later this same campaign was branded as one of the greatest failures. The explanation is to be found in the advance on Bagdad. The official and private telegrams despatched from India on the 6th and 7th October show clearly the attitude of the Government of India towards the idea of an advance upon Bagdad and their view that General Nixon's force was inadequate for the task. Had there been no exchange of telegrams on the 8th October between the Secretary of State and General Nixon it is not likely that the advance would have taken place. But when all the military authorities in London, India and Mesopotamia were in agreement that General Nixon's force was adequate for the capture of Bagdad, the advance upon it received the sanction of H.M. Government.

In consequence of the delay caused by discussion, etc., it was not till six weeks later, on the 19th November when the Turks had received reinforcements and supplies and had recovered their morale, that General Townshend fought the battle of Ctesiphon, and although the position was captured, the loss in casualties was so heavy that it was decided to retire after the evacuation of the wounded. Townshend's strategy and the gallantry of our troops was beyond all praise. Fighting a rearguard action, General Townshend reached Kut-el-Amara on the 3rd December and remained there.

From information received later, it transpired that General von der Goltz had arrived at Bagdad with heavy Turkish reinforcements and had pushed them on to Ctesiphon. The arrival of these new forces should have been ascertained by aerial reconnaissance, but Nixon neglected this precaution. I told General Nixon what I thought of this omission.

There was no news of the two additional divisions promised by H.M. Government, but the Government of India to meet the peril of the situation sent at once another division from India which could not *with safety* be spared and yet another division in a few weeks' time. In the meantime General Nixon's health had broken down and he was succeeded by General Sir Percy Lake, while General Aylmer was placed in command of the field force destined to relieve General Townshend who was invested in Kut-el-Amara. Neither of these Generals proved equal to their task, General Lake being, as Field-Marshal Robertson described him, " an Inspector General of Communications " and General Aylmer possessed no sense of strategy. In spite of the heroic gallantry of the relief force and the stubborn resistance of General Townshend, all efforts to relieve Kut proved abortive and the garrison surrendered a few weeks later. Thus ended a very regrettable incident in the Mesopotamian campaign which was only wiped out by the organization of a very large expedition which ended with the capture of Bagdad some time after I had left India.

During the course of the summer, the last I spent in Simla, I had a constant stream of visitors at Viceregal Lodge, including Ruling Princes and officials. The Maharajas of Bikaner and Gwalior were amongst them, as also the Nizam of Hyderabad for the third time and the Maharaja of Kishingahr. Bikaner was in a very unhappy frame of mind after the loss of his only daughter from phthisis. The Nizam left his wives, who insisted upon accompanying him, in a camp at the foot of the hills and came with only a small suite. He was very pleasant, but I had to remonstrate with him on his extravagance as he had practically bought the contents of the biggest jeweller's shop in Simla and distributed the contents on every side. He gave my son Alec no less than six presents and would probably have given more if I had not stopped him. Afterwards he became far too careful of his vast riches.

A new form of German intrigue showed itself in the arrival of three Americans in Calcutta, including Dr. Cook, the spurious traveller to the North Pole. Their intention was to go to Nepal, evidently with the intention of stirring up trouble on the frontier. Dr. Cook said he wished to climb mountains in the Himalayas and another of the party said he was a big-game hunter and wished to shoot. So little of a sportsman was he, that he seemed to be unaware of the fact that it was not the season for shooting big game. All three travellers were detained and deported. It transpired that Dr. Cook's father and mother were both Germans.

I must now refer to a very serious conspiracy encouraged by German money and the promise of arms and military assistance;

by which a rebellion was to be provoked by seditionists in Bengal and the Punjab on Christmas Eve 1915. The plot was run by the German General Staff with three or four seditious Indians to assist them. One of them was the brother of that Mrs. Naidu,[1] who enjoyed a certain prominence amongst Congress people in London.

It was in June 1915 that a German officer in disguise landed at Singapore and was arrested by the military authorities. Amongst his papers a map of the Bay of Bengal was found with certain marks on various points of the coast. I sent at once one of our best police officers to Singapore and after a prolonged cross-examination the German made a confession. He said that while serving on the front in Belgium he had committed an act that he would not describe for which the penalty was death, the alternative offered to him being to undertake a very dangerous mission. He had therefore been entrusted with and had undertaken a mission to organize a rebellion in Bengal and elsewhere for which both money and arms were to be supplied by the German Government from a base in the Dutch East Indies. He gave very full information of all the German plans and as proof of his bona fides he continued under our supervision to correspond with his German superiors as though he was still free and active, and on two occasions obtained from them sums of 10,000 rupees which were handed over to the Government of India. He did not wish to return to Germany or Europe and the only condition he asked was that he and his family should be smuggled over to America and that he should receive £5,000 to make a new start in life. This was promised him.

Immediate steps were taken to counteract this conspiracy. The matter was placed in the hands of the military authorities and naval patrols were organized in likely spots on the coast of Bengal with a view to intercepting the importation of arms. A ramification of the German conspiracy was discovered at Balasore in Orissa and the whole gang of conspirators was hunted down

[1] Now, in 1947, H.E. The Governor of the United Provinces.

by the police and those who were not shot were arrested. Documents found in their possession proved conclusively that they were in the German conspiracy. It was ascertained that the proposed rebellion was to take place on Christmas Day when all British military and civil authorities would be merry-making. It was therefore decided that no further step should be taken to alarm the German conspirators and that no more arrests should be made before the 15th December. Consequently all district officers were ordered to remain at their posts at Christmas and not to take their usual Christmas leave, while troop trains with troops on board were held ready at strategic points. From information given by conspirators and others, about 300 persons were arrested on the 15th December and detained while their cases were being investigated and by this prompt and decisive action the conspiracy was entirely scotched. The only failure was the penetration through our naval patrols of a ship with Germans and rifles on board, but the whereabouts of the ship and rifles was never discovered, and it was believed that the ship had been wrecked with all on board. The only force in being that was known was some German officers with a few hundred Indians in the backwoods of Burmah where they were hiding. A battalion of Ghurkas was sent to hunt them, but they escaped across the frontier into China.

The last month of my stay in Simla was an arduous one as it was an incessant round of addresses, speeches, dinner parties and a garden party at Annandale given by the Indian community. Amongst these was a dinner given me by the India Civil Service, and I made them a long speech indicating the changes that must inevitably affect their position, but pointing out that they still had a fine future before them and how they could be utilized to their own and the general advantage. It was criticized at the time but it has all come true as the India Civil Servants themselves admit.

In my speech I seized the opportunity to give expression to the feelings of admiration that I had acquired during my stay in India for the loyal and devoted attitude of the English wives and sisters of British officers and officials who, very often torn in their allegiance to their husbands or children in England, bore uncomplainingly the heat and burden of the day in the plains of India during the hot weather, very often in isolated spots where they were deprived of the society and recreation to which they were accustomed, and even, as I myself had seen on the frontier, were exposed to the risk of attack by lawless and fanatical tribesmen. Nothing could be more admirable or more conducive to the honour of the country from which they sprung. I said that from my experience in Simla the reports spread in England and elsewhere of the frivolity of the women who came to Simla and other hill stations during the hot weather were absolutely baseless. Nothing could be better than the general tone of society in Simla. I received many letters from ladies thanking me for my reference to them.

One of the functions was the presentation of my portrait to the Legislative Council room in Simla. This was a picture subscribed for by the Indian Members of the Legislative Council to the tune of £1,000 and painted by William Nicholson.[1] He stayed six months with me in Viceregal Lodge to paint it. He did two or three pictures of me, the last of which seemed satisfactory, but on my return from an absence of only two days and within four days of the sailing of Nicholson's boat for England, I found, to my surprise, a clean canvas. I was annoyed as I had to sit again to him, but he completed the picture before he left ! It was unveiled by the Pundit Malavya, of doubtful loyalty, who made a long speech eulogizing my administration, but not in very good taste as it was at the expense of my predecessors. The picture was said to be like me but in my opinion not good.

I was sorry to leave Simla for the last time, where I had spent five summers with much happiness and a great sorrow.

Towards the end of October I paid a visit to Sir James Meston, Lieutenant-Governor of the United Provinces at Naini Tal. It

[1] Now Sir William Nicholson.

is a delightful spot with a lovely lake in the cup of the mountains. The situation of Government House is precarious as the mountain is crumbling less than a hundred yards from the house.

The Lahore conspiracy gave me much trouble at this time. No less than twenty-four men were condemned to death by a Special Tribunal. I went to Lahore to see the Lieutenant-Governor, Sir M. O'Dwyer, and told him categorically that I absolutely declined to allow a holocaust of victims in a case where only six men had been proved to be actually guilty of murder and dacoity. He recommended that only six of the twenty-four should have their sentences commuted. I agreed to commutation in these cases but submitted the remaining eighteen cases to the judgment of the Law Member. He proved to me conclusively that in the case of all except six actually guilty of murder and dacoity, they had been convicted under a clause of the penal code which could not entail a death sentence. This opinion was confirmed by my Council and as there was no appeal from the Special Tribunal except to the Viceroy I had to assume the responsibility of commuting the sentences of eighteen of the twenty-four condemned to death. It was impossible on political grounds to show up publicly the mistake made by the Special Tribunal, so I had to assume full responsibility and was violently attacked in the Anglo-Indian Press for the clemency shown, but I learnt that the Calcutta Bar had detected the flaw in the judgment and were hoping that clemency would be denied, with every intention of creating a scandal and starting an agitation against Special Tribunals and the Indian " Dora ".

In November I had a good day's shooting at Bharatpur, where we got 1,700 duck to 30 guns and I spent a delightful and quiet ten days in Bikaner, where the Maharaja dispensed as usual the most friendly hospitality and where I had some very good buck and grouse shooting. I shot 26 bucks and a large number of grouse. This was the last of my many visits to Bikaner where I had always received the most generous hospitality and for whose Chief I had a genuine affection.

Christmas was spent at Gwalior with the Maharaja, one of my very best friends in India, and I took with me Diamond, who was the life and soul of the party with all the practical jokes that she and the Maharaja, who was a great baby in some ways, played on each other the whole time. She accompanied me out shooting and was present with me when I killed some tigers. I shall never forget waiting with her for a tiger near a pool on a lovely day and watching a small family of otters playing in the water a few yards from me. It was like fairyland till the tiger came and disturbed the scene to his own undoing. I shot five tigers and a bear during the visit and Alec shot his first tiger.

The year 1915 at its close proved to have been a year of exceptional anxiety in India. In addition to the campaigns carried on by Indian troops in France, Egypt, Aden, Mesopotamia and East Africa, there were, between the 29th November 1914 and the 5th September 1915, no less than seven serious attacks on the North-West Frontier, all of which were effectively dealt with. In fact, during 1915, though small attention was paid to them outside, India carried out successfully the greatest military operations on the frontier since the frontier campaign of 1897. There were also the conspiracies of Delhi and Lahore ; the efforts made by revolutionary agitators to undermine the loyalty of the Indian troops ; the return to India of the Sikh revolutionaries and the action taken against them, and finally the German conspiracy to organize rebellion in Bengal and elsewhere which was successfully scotched by the arrest of the ringleaders ten days before the plan was to mature. Nineteen-fifteen was a very anxious year in India. Still, but for the loyal attitude of the Ameer of Afghanistan it might have been a great deal worse, for no doubt a *jehad* in Afghanistan would have been very popular, the impression being that our frontier was weakly held and that on our side of the frontier there were prospects of unlimited loot. The Ameer gave me a promise of strict neutrality during the war and kept it most loyally.

At the outbreak of war with Turkey the attitude of the Ameer had been a source of some anxiety to me and the Government, since a hostile Afghanistan might have been a source of real danger to India. He lost no time, however, in sending me a secret message to the effect that he would do his utmost to maintain strict neutrality so long as the independence of Afghanistan was not threatened, but that in view of the difficulty of his position the Government of India must judge him by his deeds rather than by his words. In spite of differences of opinion in my Council, some of whom regarded this message as merely a ruse to enable the Ameer to choose his time to enter the war against us, I determined to regard his promise as being made in good faith, and when he asked me to send him the arrears of his subsidy, amounting to about a quarter of a million sterling, I agreed to do so and even increased his subsidy in order to compensate him for the extra cost of steps to be taken on the frontier to prevent raids.

The attacks made upon our frontier were by tribesmen over whom the Ameer had practically no control. Had he supported them the situation would have been extremely serious. During this time some Germans and Austrians succeeded in penetrating into Cabul. They saw the Ameer twice and pressed him to make an alliance against England, offering him even the Punjab in the event of victory. He firmly refused, stating that he would not break his alliance with the British Government. They then asked to be allowed to return to Herat, but he put guards round the garden where they were living and kept them in close confinement. When deserters from the Indian Army got into Afghanistan the Ameer would have nothing to say to them for being untrue to their salt. Before the close of the year I suggested to the King to send a letter of friendship, which His Majesty did very promptly and with splendid result as the Ameer made great capital out of it at Cabul amongst his own Sirdars and the Germans and Austrians. It was the finishing blow for the latter. There was some delay in the Ameer's reply of which the explanation is amusing. The King's letter to the Ameer was a mistake in etiquette since it was in type while it ought to have been in manuscript. The cause of the delay in the Ameer's reply to the King was that in order to act precisely in the same manner as the King had acted towards him he had at last succeeded in obtaining a Persian typewriting machine and had sent his letter in Persian type.

About two months later two letters from the Germans at Cabul were intercepted at Meshed, in both of which it was stated that there was no hope of getting the Ameer to side with them, and, in one letter it was suggested that they should proceed to extremities and organize a *coup d'état*, which meant of course the assassination of the Ameer. I promptly wrote to the Ameer giving him full information of the contents of the intercepted letters, and, as I knew him to be a man who would not run any personal risks, I expect he gave the Germans in Cabul a very poor time in consequence.

There is no doubt that the Ameer, in loyally keeping his promise of neutrality, incurred great personal difficulties, but he maintained it to the end. It was a misfortune for England and India when he was assassinated shortly after the end of the war.

A curious commentary on the situation on the frontier was that the Afridis, the largest and most warlike tribe on the frontier, gave at the New Year a large garden party at Jamrud at the entrance of the Khyber to which they invited all the officials and society of Peshawar and adjoining districts, and proved admirable hosts.

It was in September 1915 that Haig relieved Willcocks of his command of the Indian Expedition in France. It is difficult for a civilian to express an opinion on a military question, but I was informed that it had been referred to Lord Kitchener, who gave his opinion that there was no case against Willcocks. Anyhow, Haig served under me in India for more than a year as Chief of the General Staff, and I know that he was then ill-disposed towards the Indian Army, both officers and men. Willcocks belonged to the Indian Army and was adored by the men. He was a good leader and very energetic. He was succeeded by General Anderson, who commanded the Meerut division, a first-class general in every way. I was sorry for Willcocks.

From the moment of the outbreak of war with Germany the Government of India did everything in their power to meet the urgent demands of the Home Government to send troops, war material and supplies, not only to France but to East Africa, Mesopotamia, the Dardanelles, Salonica and elsewhere, but I always felt and told the Home Government my opinion that all these expeditions were, from a strategic point of view, blunders, since it was in Flanders that the war would be won and it was there that we ought to have concentrated all our efforts in order to give the Germans a smashing blow and terminate the war. All such diversions as these expeditions meant weakness in the main theatre of war and it seemed to me that we had been outwitted by Germany and were literally playing her game. There was, however, conflict of opinion in the Cabinet on the subject, various Ministers pressing for different expeditions in which their Departments were specially interested.

It was on the 1st December 1915 that the retreat to Kut commenced, and during December news began to trickle down from the Tigris to Bombay and Delhi of the insufficiency of medical supplies at the front and the consequent sufferings of the wounded. As a matter of fact there were tons of medical supplies collected at Busra, but the military authorities answered that transport was wanting. That was true, but the transport of such things as bandages and medicaments was just as important as shells and food. The story of the sufferings of the wounded was harrowing and I wrote at once to the Commander-in-Chief and instructed him to spare no effort to put these things right. It was true that the means of transport were inadequate, but then the expedition had quite unexpectedly developed in two months from two to seven divisions, and two of the new divisions from Europe arrived with only two of their six ambulances and even these without their equipment. There was undoubtedly chaotic mismanagement at Busra, the base of the expedition. With the Commander-in-Chief I decided at once to send a Mission of Inquiry and had in December actually designated Lord Chelms-ford and Surgeon-General MacNeece when the former was appointed my successor. Surgeon-General. MacNeece went, therefore, alone to Mesopotamia and made a report with which I was not satisfied. He was evidently " got round " by General Nixon, who told him that all the members of the R.A.M.C. had behaved splendidly and that there was no cause for complaint. He being an R.A.M.C. Officer himself was, naturally, only too delighted to accept this statement. This, I happened to know, actually took place. I decided therefore to send General Bingley and Sir William Vincent on a Commission of Inquiry and they eventually reported on the medical situation as being unsatisfactory in many ways. This report came in after I had left India.

It was almost a year later that I learnt for the first time of a report received by the Army Department in Delhi of the deplorable condition of about 100 wounded soldiers who had been put on board a barge at Kut and who had made the journey to Busra without medical comforts or accommodation and with insufficient medical attendance. Although none had died during the journey they were in a bad state on their arrival, while the condition of the barge was appalling. These men had been hastily crowded on the barge, several other barges having been sunk by gun-fire, in order to save them from extermination by the Arabs, who were following up the retirement of our troops after the battle of Ctesiphon. Of course it was very sad that these brave men should have been subjected to so much suffering and discomfort, but in a retreat this state of affairs is almost inevitable, and surely it is better they should be crowded on board any kind of boat than that they should have had their throats cut by the Arabs. My complaint is that, as I ascertained, this report was received by the Army Department and was not sent to me, as was usual in such cases. In fact, I have never yet seen that report though I have heard much of its contents.

It was only in February 1916 that the War Office took over the general control of operations in Mesopotamia, and for the first time during the war the campaign in Mesopotamia, which had been regarded as the Cinderella of the campaigns in progress, India having at the outset of the war in Europe given everything to England from her reserves, was treated with long-awaited generosity. Had this policy been adopted earlier the situation at this time might have been very different. Troops, drafts, aeroplanes, guns and transport were poured into Mesopotamia, but unfortunately it was too late to save the garrison of Kut.

It was at this time that I heard that Miss Gertrude Bell, whom I had known many years before as the niece of Sir Frank Lascelles, and who was employed in the Military Intelligence Department at Cairo, was ill and unhappy on account of the death of a very great friend in the operations at Gallipoli. I asked her to come to pay me a visit at Delhi, where she would have an opportunity of studying the Arab information at the disposal of the Foreign Department. She came and stayed some weeks at Viceregal Lodge, and being much impressed with the information on Arabia collected by the Foreign Department, I suggested to her, and she accepted the idea, that I should send her to Busra to join the staff of Sir Percy Cox, our High Commissioner. I warned her that being a woman her presence would be resented by Sir Percy, but that it rested with her by her tact and knowledge to make good her position. As I anticipated, there was serious opposition at Busra, but as is well known she, by her ability and her obvious good sense and tact, overcame it and remained there for some years, occupying an important Staff post until her death. She was a very nice and most remarkable woman, but she never fell in love till she was 50 !

CHAPTER IX

LAST MONTHS IN INDIA, 1916

THREE months before I left India the Gaekwar of Baroda realized at last how very unsatisfactory his attitude towards the Government had been during the five years I had been in India, and wishing to wipe the slate clean, wrote me a repentant letter, asking my forgiveness and promising better behaviour. I replied, freely forgiving him and expressing the hope that he would never create any more friction between himself and the Government of India. I asked him to pay me a visit at Delhi, which he did. From reports that I have since heard he really turned over a new leaf.

The period of the last three months before I left India was a very strenuous time, for in addition to my ordinary routine work I had ceremonies to perform, visits to make and farewell addresses to receive.

At the beginning of February I spent two days in Bankipore. The new city had grown wonderfully and gave promise of being very fine. I opened the new High Court of Justice, the coping-stone of the new province of my creation, and the finest High Court in India. It was an immense satisfaction to me to be able to take part in this ceremony before leaving India.

From Bankipore I went on to Benares to lay the foundation-stone of the Hindu University. It was a very big function and a very successful one. Being a purely Indian function, it was in great contrast to the ceremony at Bankipore of the day before, which was purely official. The Durbar at Benares was extraordinarily picturesque with the Ruling Chiefs and all the Indians in their smartest clothes, in bright colours and parti-coloured turbans. A most picturesque sight. There were 6,000 people present and all very enthusiastic. It was a great effort for me as

I had a temperature of 103 the night before and only got out of bed to go to the ceremony, but I got through the whole programme, including luncheon with the Maharaja, and made a speech at the foundation ceremony lasting half an hour which was well received. Immediately after the close of the Durbar I went to my train and remained in bed till I reached Delhi.

There had been some excitement as to the line I would take towards Mrs. Besant, who was to be there and who had on occasions been frankly seditious, but whom I had always been careful to ignore. The Maharaja apologized to me for her presence, but I merely said, " Who is Mrs. Besant ? " and at the reception shook hands with her as with everybody else.

The preceding six months had been for me a time of very anxious stress, far more anxious than anybody could have any idea of. Had I been able to return to England at the end of the usual term of five years my health would not have been impaired. But during the additional six months that I stayed in India at the request of the Government, my health steadily deteriorated and I became subject to attacks of fever which I had not had before in India. It was a reminder that after more than five years in India without return to England my powers of resistance to the Indian climate were becoming weaker and that a change was necessary. Still, the damage was not serious nor permanent.

Towards the end of February I went to Jodhpur to invest the young Maharaja of Jodhpur with full powers in open Durbar. It was a fine sight to see such a gathering of splendidly good-looking Rajputs from all Rajputana, and the people seemed very pleased. But I think the happiest was that splendid old man Sir Pertab Singh who saw his task as Regent satisfactorily concluded. My impression was that the young Maharaja would do well, but alas, like his father, he fell a victim to drink and died in a very few years. The number of Ruling Princes who have died from drink is sadly deplorable.

In the early stages of the war all Germans with their families in India were interned in various internment camps, where they lived a life not of luxury but of comfort. It was decided later between the British and German Governments that women and children in internment camps in either country should be returned to their native homes. Consequently we received instructions from the Home Government to charter a ship and to send home, via the Cape, where a further batch of Germans was to be collected, all the German women and children in India. This was just at the moment when the Germans were pursuing a policy of " frightfulness " with their submarines, and they actually had the impertinence to ask us to put some distinguishing mark on the vessel so that they might not torpedo it by mistake ! Of course this was refused, but as I was leaving India for England about six weeks later I took the opportunity to place all my heavy baggage on board this ship, being certain that with this cargo of German women on board the vessel would not be sunk. It reached its destination in safety.

Before I left India I had the satisfaction of achieving three objects which gave me and others intense satisfaction.

In the first place I opened the Lady Hardinge Medical College and Hospital for women at Delhi which had been initiated by my wife and funds collected by her to the amount of more than £100,000, with additional promises of annual subscriptions amounting to nearly £1,500 per annum. The need of such a college was imperative since, in most Indian castes, women can only be treated by women and the numbers that died annually from the ignorant treatment of unskilled and untrained midwives, etc., was quite appalling. The Indian public realized this and the moment the proposal was started subscriptions and support of every kind poured in so as to make it a success. It was the first college of its kind for women to be established in India, and its success from the day of its opening has been phenomenal in its rapid development and in the number of female doctors with medical degrees that it has turned out. The hospital attached to it has always been overflowing. It is the finest memorial that any woman could have.

Secondly, I was very pleased to have secured from the Home Government the promise that Indian indentured labour for the colonies should be abolished. I had always heard rumours of the sufferings and degradation of indentured Indians in plantations in our colonies and I deputed Mr. MacNeil, an able Indian Civil Servant, and later President of the Irish Free State, to undertake a Mission of Inquiry into the position of indentured Indians in British colonies. His report confirmed my apprehensions and I never ceased to press the Home Government to give me a definite assurance that this form of servitude or even slavery, should be abolished. This concession I obtained a few weeks before I left India.

The third object that I attained was an assurance from the Home Government that as soon as the war was over the economic position of India would be reconsidered with a view to abolishing the excise duty on cotton. This excise duty on cotton goods was imposed on India as a protective measure for the cotton industries of Lancashire and it certainly exposed the British Government to the accusation that India was being governed in the interests of Lancashire rather than of India. To this reproach there was absolutely no reply and I felt its injustice so keenly that I left no stone unturned during my term of office in India to obtain its removal.

I was able to announce both these concessions during the last few sittings of the Legislative Assembly before my departure and they were received with the utmost enthusiasm all over India. Nothing could have been more appreciated.

It was on the 9th March that I received a telegram from the Secretary of State saying that in recognition of my services in India the King had been pleased to confer upon me the Order of the Garter. To me it was one of the greatest surprises of my life, for I had never expected to receive so high an honour, and moreover it had never before been given to anybody of less rank than a viscount. It was a curious fact that in the cypher telegram to me recording the fact, the only word omitted was that of

" Garter " and I had to telegraph to have the telegram repeated, though I had a shrewd guess as to what the omission was since there was no other Knighthood that could be offered to me. There was no mark of approval that I would have preferred and I was enchanted. It was announced publicly on the 24th March which happened to be the last day of the session of the Legislative Assembly and the last day upon which, after 5½ years as President, I could preside.

While the sitting was in progress I noticed what was evidently a Reuter's telegram being passed round amongst the Members and during an interval in the Debate the Vice-President, Sir William Clark, rose and on behalf of the Assembly offered me their congratulations. There was a tremendous demonstration and the cheers lasted for some minutes. Congratulations poured in on every side and everybody seemed as pleased as I was.

My last meeting of the Legislative Assembly was, however, a very trying performance. After a long debate on the Budget I wound up the session and bade farewell to the Members in a speech which lasted 55 minutes. It was very exhausting as it was very hot. In spite of the fact that I took the opportunity to tell the Indian Members some home truths, it was very well received, and one of the most advanced Indian Members told me afterwards that this plain speaking was badly needed and would, in his opinion, do a great deal of good. It is interesting now to look back on the fact, now that "Dominion Status" had been declared by Lord Irwin,[1] when Viceroy, as the ultimate goal of political development in India, that I endeavoured to impress upon the Imperial Legislative Council that the self-governing institutions existing in the Dominions had been achieved not by a sudden stroke of statesmanship but by a process of steady and patient evolution. I pointed out that in India it was not idealism that was needed but practical solutions, and that India should look facts squarely in the face and do her utmost to

[1] Afterwards Earl of Halifax.

grapple with realities. In spite of Lord Irwin's declaration I believe that these sentiments are still in the main true.

My last few days in Delhi were spent in receiving deputations to bid farewell and in giving farewell audiences, and I left Delhi for Bombay on the last day of March, my successor being due to arrive on the 4th April. The whole of Delhi came to Viceregal Lodge to say good-bye and it was a trying performance as so many people did so with tears running down their cheeks, amongst them being the Commander-in-Chief.

The two days I spent in Bombay with the Willingdons were very full. 'I received several addresses to which I had to reply, but an honour of exceptional interest was paid to me by the conferment at the University of Bombay of an honorary degree of Doctor of Laws. No other Viceroy had received this honour since Lord Ripon thirty-two years earlier. Bombay was also full of Maharajas, all of whom I had to receive in separate audiences.

When Lord Chelmsford arrived on the 4th April I received him on the steps of Government House and welcomed him. After lunching together with the Willingdons I left for the harbour through dense crowds who cheered me all the way. On the Apollo Bunder the *shamiana* was filled to its utmost capacity with all the official classes of Bombay and no less than thirty-five Maharajas who had come from their states to see me off. I received an address from the Bombay Municipal Corporation and in my reply I was so affected by my surroundings and the circumstances of my departure that I very nearly broke down, but I heard afterwards that my speech was considered to be one of the best I had made in India. I was fond of Bombay, which I had visited no less than six times and the people were always friendly and encouraging. My statue stands on the Apollo Bunder, raised by Bombay and adjoining the Gate of India, the only others being those of the King and Queen.

My farewells were very trying. All the Princes and many others wept, and I was glad when I got on board the P. & O.

S.S. *Arabia* and able to take leave quietly of those of my staff who were not returning with me. I was worn out and slept for nearly two days after weighing anchor.

My Private Secretary, Sir James Du Boulay, with Lady Du Boulay and two daughters, returned home with me, having served with me during the whole of my time in India, and without a single day's leave from duty. I would like to place here on record my profound gratitude to Sir James Du Boulay for his most able and loyal services to me. He was extraordinarily helpful and understanding, and inspired confidence in all those who came into contact and had to deal with him. The life of a Viceroy is always nerve-racking and it is difficult not to become irritable at times, but, as I explained to him once when he felt I had been unduly critical, I looked upon him as my safety-valve, so that I could sometimes let off steam when the pressure of irritation from outside sources became more than one could bear, but that it meant nothing. He accepted this and during $5\frac{1}{2}$ years we never had any difference of any kind, even if our views on any particular subject were not in entire agreement. He was extremely hardworking, and in fact a perfect private secretary, delightful companion and true friend. Lady Du Boulay was also extremely kind to my little daughter when deprived of her mother's love and help.

It seemed strange to me to suddenly snap my relations with India on which my thoughts had been entirely concentrated for $5\frac{1}{2}$ years, but it was a source of satisfaction to me that I was able to hand over my charge to my successor with the knowledge that India, in spite of twenty months of war, was absolutely quiet and loyal. Everybody was of opinion that for many years past India had not been so free from agitation and trouble as then, and I was truly able to say that the situation was infinitely better than when I first arrived in India. The Government and people had come closer and there was a feeling of confidence between them which was of recent growth.

My journey home with Alec and Diamond was comparatively

uneventful. When our ship stopped at Suez I was surprised and greatly touched by receiving a visit from General Sir Charles Davis, who was in command there. Some years previously he had been in the Military Intelligence Department where I had learnt to appreciate his merit and his value as a perfect German scholar, and when I heard that he was about to be retired as a Senior Major in the Guards I protested to Lord Haldane, who promptly gave him a Staff appointment of which he had made such good use as to become a General during the war. We disembarked at Suez, and went to Ismailia, where I met General Sir Archibald Murray, who was in command on the Canal, and from there we went to Cairo and stayed one night at the Residency before proceeding to Port Said to rejoin our ship. All the Indian troops stationed along the Canal turned out and cheered me as I passed them in a launch.

As it was known that the ship on which I was to return to England would receive special protection it was crowded with women and children. In passing through the danger zone of German submarines our ship steamed very fast and without lights, nobody knowing the danger except the Captain and myself. All the women and children slept on deck in the Mediterranean.

At Dover I was welcomed by the Mayor and Corporation and at Victoria Station by Lord Farquhar on behalf of the King, and by a deputation from the Foreign Office with other friends. When all this was over it was a great joy and relief to feel that I had no further responsibility and that I was a nobody once more.

INDEX

INDEX

147

INDEX

Nixon, General, 120, 122–5, 135
Northumberland Fusiliers, 95
North-West Frontier, 70, 102, 107, 116, 131–3 .
Nunn, Captain W., 120

O'Dwyer, Sir Michael, 116, 130
Opium, 40, 93
Orissa, 127 (*see also* Behar and Orissa)
Orissa Tenancy and Mining Law, 68–9

Palanpur, Nawab of, 119
Pathans, 108
Patiala, 69
Patna, 38, 92
Penshurst, 13
Pentland, 1st Lord, 63
Persian Gulf, 111, 114
Persian Oil Company, 112
Pertab Singh, General Sir, 34, 93–4, 138 .
Peshawar, 69, 133
Poonch, Maharaja of, 49
Port Said, 7–8, 144
Power, M., 24–5
Punjab, 25, 56, 79, 116, 127

Quetta, 25–6

Radnor, 6th Earl of, 107
Rajputana, 57, 138
Ranjit Singh, 25
Reay, 11th Lord, 66
Rewah, Maharaja of, 95, 103
Ripon, 2nd Marquess of, 118, 142
Robertson, Sir Benjamin, 63, 92
Ronaldshay, Earl of (2nd Marquess of Zetland), 56
Roos-Keppel, Sir G., 69, 115
Russia, 6, 31

Sabathu, 95–6
Samana, 69–70

Sazonow, M., 6
Scindia, Maharaja of Gwalior, 35, 56, 86, 90, 126, 131
"Servants of India Society," 115
Shaiba, 113, 120, 123
Shatt-el-Arab, 102, 112
Shaukat Ali, 117
Shinwari tribe, 69
Sikhs, 24–5, 116, 117, 131
Simla, 20, 27–9, 42, 71, 73, 86–7, 95–6, 126, 128–9
Singapore, 127
Slacke, Mr., 35
Slade, Admiral Sir Edmund, 9, 44–5
Smuts, Field-Marshal, 91–2
South African Indians, 90–2, 115
Southborough, 1st Lord, 63
Stamfordham, Lord, 18, 39, 46
Suffolk, 19th Earl of, 107
Sukkhur Bridge, 27 .
Surveillance Bill, 96
Swinton, Captain G., 67

Tonk, Nawab of, 76–7
Townshend, General Sir C., 120, 123–6
Turkey and Turks, 102, 117, 120, 131

Udaipur, Maharana of, 74–5, 86
United Provinces, 87, 100, 121

Victor Emmanuel III, King of Italy, 8
Vincent, Sir William, 135

West Kent Regiment, 12
Willcocks, General Sir W., 31, 100, 133–4
Willingdon, Lord and Lady (afterwards Marquess and Marchioness of), 109, 119, 142
William, Crown Prince, 19
William II, German Emperor, 20
Wilson, Sir Guy Fleetwood, 16

150

Date Due

CAT. NO. 23 233   PRINTED IN U.S.A.

CPSIA information can be obtained
at www.ICGtesting.com
Printed in the USA
BVHW042323150223
658636BV00018B/216